In Sync 1

Ingrid Freebairn
Jonathan Bygrave
Judy Copage

PEARSON
Longman

Contents

Contents

Contents

Contents

Grammar	The verb *be*: singular
	Subject pronouns: *I, you, he, she, it*
	Possessive adjectives: *my, your, his, her, its*
Vocabulary	Numbers 1–100
Function	Talk about yourself and others

Get started

1 Look at the photo. Where are the people? What do you think a youth club is? Would you like to join one?

Presentation

2 Listen and read along. Who's the youth coordinator?

David: Hi, Polly. How are you?

Polly: Fine, thanks. And you?

David: I'm OK, thanks. This is my sister, Laura.

Polly: Hi, Laura. Nice to meet you. Is it your first time here?

Laura: Yes, it is. What's that?

Polly: It's my new cell phone.

Laura: Cool ring tone!

Polly: Thanks.

Zach: Hi, guys!

Laura: Who's he?

David: He's the youth coordinator. His name's Zach.

Laura: How old is he?

David: I don't know. 20? 25?

Carlos: Hi, guys. How are things? What's that sound?

Polly: Oh, it's my cell phone again.

Carlos: Weird ring tone!

Phrases

 Listen and repeat.

- Nice to meet you.
- How are you?
- This is [my sister].
- Thanks.

💡 Solve it!

3 Listen again. Write the names of the people in the photo.

Vocabulary: Numbers 1–100

4  Listen and repeat.

1 one	11 eleven	21 twenty-one
2 two	12 twelve	30 thirty
3 three	13 thirteen	40 forty
4 four	14 fourteen	50 fifty
5 five	15 fifteen	60 sixty
6 six	16 sixteen	70 seventy
7 seven	17 seventeen	80 eighty
8 eight	18 eighteen	90 ninety
9 nine	19 nineteen	100 a hundred/ one hundred
10 ten	20 twenty	

LUNCH SPECIALS
Sandwiches $3
Burgers $4
Soda 90¢

A

5 Find six numbers in the photo and say them.

PARKSIDE
YOUTH
CLUB

22

55

D

E *Carlos*

B

C

Presentation

6 🎧 [1 05] Listen and read along. How old are David, Polly, and Laura?

> **1** Carlos: Hello. My name**'s** Carlos.
> Zach: Hi, Carlos. **Are** you a new member?
> Carlos: Yes, I **am**.
> David: It**'s** his first time here.

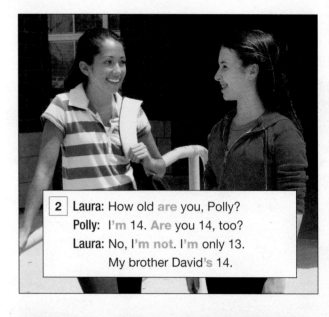

> **2** Laura: How old **are** you, Polly?
> Polly: I**'m** 14. **Are** you 14, too?
> Laura: No, I**'m not**. I**'m** only 13.
> My brother David**'s** 14.

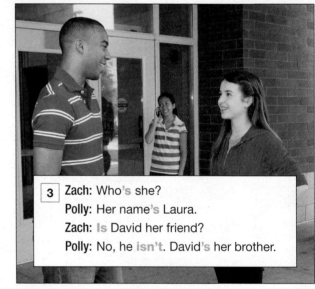

> **3** Zach: Who**'s** she?
> Polly: Her name**'s** Laura.
> Zach: **Is** David her friend?
> Polly: No, he **isn't**. David**'s** her brother.

Grammar

The verb *be*: singular

Affirmative	Negative
I'm 13.	I'm not 14.
You're 13.	You aren't 14.
He/She's 13.	He/She isn't 14.
It's new.	It isn't old.

Questions	Short answers
Am I 13?	Yes, you are. / No, you aren't.
Is he/she 15?	Yes, he/she is. / No, he/she isn't.
Is it new?	Yes, it is. / No, it isn't.
How old are you?	I'm 13.
Who's he?	He's the youth coordinator.

☞ Go to page 128, Master your grammar.

Practice

7 Complete the chart.

Long Form	Short Form (Contractions)
I am	*I'm*
	You're
He is	
	She's
It is	
	What's
Who is	

Practice

8 Complete the sentences.

> • is (x3) • 's • isn't • am (x2)
> • 'm • are • aren't

1 What <u>'s</u> _____ number one?

2 How old _____ Laura?

3 Hi. I _____ Michael and
this _____ Sarah.

4 A: _____ you 14?
  B: Yes, I _____ .

5 A: _____ it a new cell
  phone?
  B: No, it _____ .

6 A: _____ I right?
  B: No, you _____ .

9 Rewrite the conversations in
your notebook using contractions
where possible.

1 A: <u>What is</u> that? *What's that?*
  B: <u>It is</u> a photo of my sister.
  A: <u>What is</u> her name?
  B: <u>It is</u> Alice.

2 A: How old are you?
  B: <u>I am</u> 11.
  A: No, <u>you are not</u>. <u>You are</u> 12.

3 A: Is that your cell phone?
  B: No, <u>it is not</u>.

10a Complete the conversation
with your information.

Q: What's your name?

You: _____

Q: How old are you?

You: _____

b PAIRS Practice the conversation
with a partner.

Pronunciation:
/ɪ/ f<u>i</u>fty

11 🎧 Go to page 126.

Grammar

Subject pronouns	Possessive adjectives
I	my
you	your
he	his
she	her
it	its

☞ Go to page 128, Master your grammar.

Speak

12a Role-play a conversation
with one of these famous people.
Use Exercise 10a as a model.

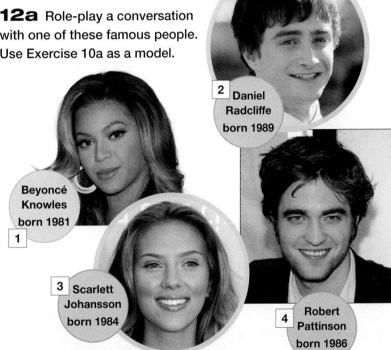

1 Beyoncé Knowles born 1981

2 Daniel Radcliffe born 1989

3 Scarlett Johansson born 1984

4 Robert Pattinson born 1986

b GROUPS One student describes a person in Exercise 12a.
The group members guess their last names!

He's 22 years old. He's an actor. His first name is Daniel.

Write

13 On a piece of paper, write about yourself and your best
friend. Use these questions for ideas.

What's your name?   What's your best friend's name?
How old are you?   How old is he or she?

 Extra practice
 • Student Book, page 112, Lesson 1A
 • Language Builder: WB, page 2; GB, page 100
 • Student CD-ROM, Unit 1

What's your address?

Vocabulary	The alphabet
	Days of the week
Function	Give personal information
	Greet people and say good-bye

Get started

1 When someone asks for your address, what information do you give?

Presentation

2 🔊 ₀₇ Listen and read along. What is Laura's home phone number?

Zach: Hi, Mrs. Miles. Laura, come in and register with Mrs. Miles.
Mrs. Miles: Hello. What's your name?
Laura: Laura Guzman.
Mrs. Miles: How do you spell Guzman?
Laura: G-U-Z-M-A-N.
Mrs. Miles: And what's your address?
Laura: It's 37 Pike Street, Seattle, Washington. That's P-I-K-E.
Mrs. Miles: And your ZIP code?
Laura: It's 98112.
Mrs. Miles: OK. Now what's your home phone number?
Laura: It's (206) 555–8127.
Mrs. Miles: Thank you, Laura. You're all done.

Comprehension

3 Complete the form for Laura.

Parkside Youth Club

Registration form for new members

Last name: _____

First name: _____

Address: _____

_____

ZIP code: _____

Home phone number: _____

💡 Solve it!

4 Look at the photo below. What day is it tomorrow?

TUESDAY
23
AUGUST

Vocabulary: The alphabet

5a 🎧 ¹/₀₈ Listen and repeat.

Aa	Ee	Ii	Mm	Qq	Uu	Yy
Bb	Ff	Jj	Nn	Rr	Vv	Zz
Cc	Gg	Kk	Oo	Ss	Ww	
Dd	Hh	Ll	Pp	Tt	Xx	

b 🎧 ¹/₀₉ Write the letters from Exercise 5a in the correct group (same vowel sound). Then listen and check.

```
1  B  C _ _ _ _ _ _ _
2  F  L _ _ _ _ _
3  A  _ _ _
4  Q  _ _
5  I  _
```

Practice

6 Spell your first and last name.

Listen

7 🎧 ¹/₁₀ Listen and complete the form.

Parkside Youth Club

Registration form for new members

Last name: _____

First name: _____

Address: _____

_____

ZIP code: _____

Home phone number: _____

Vocabulary: Days of the week

8a 🎧 ¹/₁₁ Listen and repeat.

Weekdays: • Monday • Tuesday
• Wednesday • Thursday • Friday
The weekend: • Saturday • Sunday

b What day is it today? _____
What day is it tomorrow? _____

Use your English: Greet people and say good-bye

9 🎧 ¹/₁₂ **PAIRS** Listen and repeat. Then practice the conversation.

Carlos:	Good morning, Mr. Davis.
Mr. Davis:	Good morning, Carlos. How are you?
Carlos:	Fine, thanks. And you?
Mr. Davis:	Not bad, thanks. See you on Friday.
Carlos:	Bye.

Greet people	**Respond**
• Hi./Hello.	• Hi./Hello.
• Good morning.	• Good morning.
• How are you?	• Fine, thanks.
How are you doing?	How are you?
• How are things?	• Ok, thanks.
	• Not bad, thanks.
	• I'm good, thanks.

Say good-bye
• Bye./Good-bye.
• See you (later)./See you on (Friday).
• Goodnight.

Write

10 Research the ways that people in the U.S. greet each other and ask "How are you?" On a piece of paper, write a list.

 Extra practice
• **Student Book, page 112, Lesson 1B**
• **Language Builder: WB, page 4**
• **Student CD-ROM, Unit 1**

Where are you from?

Grammar	The verb *be*: plural
	Subject pronouns: *we, you, they*
Vocabulary	Countries and nationalities
Function	Talk about countries and nationalities

A

Ciao!

Get started

1 Can you guess the corresponding nationalities for these countries?

Brazil   Chile   Mexico
the U.K.   the U.S.

¡Hola!

B

Read

2 [1 13] Listen and read along. Write the letter of each photo next to the correct conversation.

1
- Excuse me. Where **are** you from?
- We**'re** from Poland. We**'re** Polish.
- **Are** you from Warsaw?
- Yes, we **are**.

2
- Excuse me. **Are** you from Brazil?
- No, we **aren't**. We**'re** from Mexico.
- Oh. Where **are** you from in Mexico?
- We**'re** from Mexico City.

C

Cześć!

3
- What's their nationality?
- They**'re** Italian.
- **Are** they from Rome?
- No, they **aren't**. They**'re** from Milan.

Vocabulary: Countries and nationalities

3 [1 14] Match the countries to the numbers on the map.

_5_ Argentina __ Australia __ Brazil __ Canada
__ Chile __ China __ France __ Greece
__ Italy __ Japan __ Madagascar __ Mexico
__ Poland __ Portugal __ Russia __ Spain
__ Sudan __ Turkey __ the U.K. __ the U.S.

4 Write the nationality adjective for each country in Exercise 3 in the correct group.

1 -an/-ian	2 -ish	3 -ese	4 other
Argentinian	*Polish*	*Chinese*	*French*

Pronunciation: Word stress

5 🎧 Go to page 126.

Grammar

The verb *be*: plural	
Affirmative	**Negative**
We/You/They**'re** from Mexico.	We/You/They **aren't** from Brazil.
Questions	**Short answers**
Are we/you/they from Brazil?	Yes, we/you/they **are**. No, we/you/they **aren't**.
Where are you from?	Mexico.

☞ Go to page 128, Master your grammar.

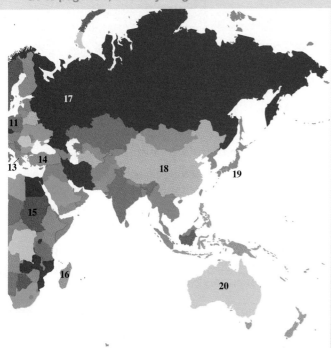

Practice

6a Complete the sentences with *are* or *aren't*.

1 The U.K. and China ____*aren't*____ on the same continent.
2 The U.S. and Canada _____ in North America.
3 Brazil and Argentina _____ the biggest South American countries.
4 The U.S. and Brazil _____ in Europe.
5 Australia and Canada _____ English-speaking countries.
6 Canada and the U.K. _____ Spanish-speaking countries.

b In your notebook, change the sentences in Exercise 6a into *yes / no* questions.

1 Are the U.K. and China on the same continent?

Speak

7 PAIRS Take turns asking and answering the questions in Exercise 6b.

A: *Are the U.K. and China on the same continent?*
B: *No, they aren't. The U.K. is in Europe, and China is in Asia.*

8 GROUPS Do you know what countries these people are from? Take turns. Ask and answer *where* questions.

A: *Where are the Black-eyed Peas from?*
B: *They're from the U.S. They're American.*

> • Black-eyed Peas • Daniel Radcliffe • Ziyi Zhang
> • Salma Hayek • Penelope Cruz • Kaka

Write

9 Think of five famous people from different countries. Write three sentences saying where they're from and their nationalities.

Laura Chinchilla is president of Costa Rica. She's from San José, Costa Rica. She's Costa Rican.

> ◉ **Extra practice**
> • Student Book, page 112, Lesson 1C
> • Language Builder: WB, page 6; GB, page 101
> • Student CD-ROM, Unit 1

English around the world

Curriculum link: Geography

Get started

1 Test your knowledge. Name three English-speaking countries.

Read

2 Now take the Geography quiz, Part 1 and Part 2. Then check your answers to Part 1. The key is at the bottom of the page.

Geography quiz

Part 1: Label the photos (1–4) with the letter of the correct English-speaking country.

A Canada   B New Zealand   C the U.K.   D the U.S.
E the Republic of Ireland F Australia   G South Africa

Part 2: Read the text "World English" quickly. Then answer these questions.

1 How many countries are there in the world?

_____

2 In how many countries is English the official language?

_____

3 What is the second language of the U.S.?

_____

4 What are the official languages of Canada?

_____

3 Read the text. Check your answers to Part 2 of the quiz.

New words
- world • geography • quiz
- English-speaking • official
- language • second
- more than • important
- some • only • for example
- other • several

World English

There are about 193 countries in the world. English is the official language in more than 45 countries.

In the U.S. there isn't an official language, but English is the first language and Spanish is an important second language.

In some countries, for example, in Australia and in the U.K., English is the only official language.

In other countries, there are several official languages. In Canada, they are English and French. In South Africa, English is one of 11 official languages!

Quiz answers to Part 1: 1 Canada
2 the U.K. 3 the U.S. 4 Australia

10

Learning strategy: Scan for information

When you want to find specific information in a text, you **scan** it. When you scan, you don't need to read every word. For example, to find names, places, countries, nationalities, and languages in a text, look for words that begin with capital letters.

Comprehension

4 Scan the web article and complete column 1 in the chart.

www.worldenglish.net — □☐✕

File Edit View Favorites Tools Help

worldenglish.net

Who are you?

My name's Santiago Perez. I'm from Buenos Aires, in Argentina. Buenos Aires is a very big city. I speak Spanish. My second language is English.

Why is English important for you?

English is important for me for three reasons:

1 The Internet is great for school projects and homework, and many websites on the Internet are in English.
2 English is the language of student chat rooms. My student chat room friends are in Argentina, Spain, Russia, Italy, and the U.S.
3 English is important for many jobs in Argentina.

	1	2
First name:	*Santiago*	*Celine*
Last name:		
Nationality:		
City and country:		
Languages:		

5 Now read the web article carefully. Write *T* for *true* or *F* for *false*. Underline the false information.

___T___ 1 Santiago's hometown is big.
_____ 2 Santiago's first language is English.
_____ 3 The Internet is important for school work.
_____ 4 Santiago's student chat room conversations are in Spanish.
_____ 5 English isn't important for jobs in Argentina.

Listen

6a 🎧 Listen to Celine's podcast. Complete column 2 of the chart in Exercise 4.

b 🎧 Listen again. Write one reason why English is important for Celine.

_____

_____

Speak

7 GROUPS Discuss: Why is English important for you? Make notes listing your group's reasons.

Write

8 On a piece of paper, write about why English is important for you. Start your paragraph by giving your name and where you're from. Use Santiago's text to help you.

CLIL PROJECT, page 140

Your life

What are these?

Grammar	Indefinite article: *a/an*
	Regular nouns: plural
	This, that, these, those
Vocabulary	Common objects
Function	Talk about everyday objects

Get started

1 Name as many of the items in the photo as you can.

Vocabulary: Common objects

2 🎧 1/17 Match the objects in the photo (1–15) to the words in the box. Then listen, check, and repeat.

___ apple ___ bag/backpack ___ books ___ camera
___ hat ___ ID card ___ keys ___ cell phone
___ MP3 player ___ notebook ___ pen
___ sandwiches ___ sneakers ___ T-shirt ___ watch

Presentation

3 🎧 1/18 Listen and read along. Circle the names of objects.

Laura: What's that? Is it a new backpack?

David: Yes, it is. Hey! Where's my MP3 player?

Laura: I don't know.

David: I think it's in my backpack. Oh, no! It isn't here!

Laura: What's this? Is this it?

David: Yes, that's it. Great! Thanks.

Polly: What are these?

David: They're my sneakers.

Polly: Your sneakers? Yuck! They're disgusting! They look ten years old.

David: Don't be silly! What are those?

Polly: Banana and chicken sandwiches.

David: Now those are really disgusting!

(Phrases)

🎧 1 19 **Listen and repeat.**

• Don't be silly! • I don't know.
• Yuck! • Great!

Grammar

Indefinite article: *a/an*		Regular nouns: plural	
Singular		**Plural**	
a pen		pens	
a sandwich		sandwiches	
an apple		apples	

☞ Go to page 129, Master your grammar.

Practice

4 Write the words from Exercise 2 in the correct column.

a	*an*	plural
a cell phone	an orange T-shirt	keys

Pronunciation: /ə/ camer<u>a</u>

5 🎧 Go to page 126.

Speak

6 PAIRS Ask and answer questions about what's in your bag.

A: *What's in your bag?*

B: *A notebook, two apples, . . .*

Grammar

This, that, these, those

What's **this**?
It's a pen.

What are **these**?
They're books.

What's **that**?
It's an MP3 player.

What are **those**?
They're keys.

☞ Go to page 129, Master your grammar.

Practice

7 Ask and answer questions about objects 1–6 below.

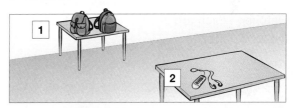

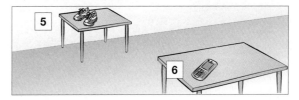

Write

8 Exchange backpacks with your partner. On a piece of paper, write a list of the items in your partner's backpack using *a*, *an*, or the plural form.

an apple, a pen, books . . .

> **Extra practice**
> • **Student Book, page 113, Lesson 2A**
> • **Language Builder: WB, page 10; GB, page 103**
> • **Student CD-ROM, Unit 2**

Grammar	Possessive *'s* (singular) and *s'* (plural)
	Possessive adjectives: *our, your, their*
Vocabulary	Colors
Function	Talk about important things in your life

Get started

1 What is important in your life? Number these things in order: 1 = very important, 5 = not very important.

- ☐ pets
- ☐ friends
- ☐ music
- ☐ sports
- ☐ possessions
- ☐ family

Read

2 🎧 1 22 Listen and read along about Danny Fletcher. Which topics from Exercise 1 are on the web page?

Comprehension

3 Read the web page again and complete the profile for Danny.

Profile

1 What's your name?	*Danny Fletcher*
2 Where are you from?	
3 What's important in your life?	
4 Who are your best friends?	
5 What's your favorite possession?	
6 What's your favorite band?	

Speak

4 **PAIRS** Interview each other. Use the questions from Exercise 3.

whatsimportant.com

Home	Search	My Profile	Chat	Help

What's important in your life?

Username: Danny99

Hi. I'm Danny Fletcher. I'm from Seattle.

So what's important in my life? My friends are very important! This is a photo of me with Carla and Rob, my best friends. We're at Carla's house. Carla's wearing a green T-shirt and Rob's wearing a yellow and black T-shirt. Carla's sister, Emily, is wearing a white T-shirt. The dog's name is Brutus. It's their parents' dog.

My cell phone is also very important to me. All my friends' phone numbers are in my phone.

Music is also important in my life. My favorite band is Green Day. Their new album is great. Rob, Carla, and I are in a band. Our band is called Purple Apples. That's Rob's blue and black guitar in the photo.

Grammar

Possessive *'s* (singular)	Possessive *s'* (plural)
Rob**'s** guitar Carla**'s** sister	their parents**'** dog my friends**'** phone numbers

☞ Go to page 129, Master your grammar.

Practice

5 Complete the sentences using the word in parentheses and possessive *'s* or possessive *s'*.

1 That's ___*David's*___ (David) cell phone.
2 She's my _____ (parents) friend.
3 What's your _____ (friends) band called?
4 I'm _____ (Tony) brother.
5 This is the _____ (boys) favorite band.

Grammar

Subject pronouns	Possessive adjectives
we	our
you	your
they	their

☞ Go to page 128, Master your grammar.

Practice

6 Complete with *our, your,* or *their*.

1 We're in ___*our*___ new house.
2 They're late. What's _____ phone number?
3 This is a photo of us at _____ school.
4 **A:** Hi, you two! Are they _____ dogs?
  B: Yes, they are. _____ names are Benji and Rufus.

Vocabulary: Colors

7a (1 23) Match a color to a number. Then listen, check, and repeat.

__ beige __ black __ blue __ brown
__ green __ gray __ orange __ pink
__ purple __ red _1_ white __ yellow

1	2	3	4	5	6
7	8	9	10	11	12

b Write the color for each.

Danny's shirt ___*red*___   Emily's shirt _____

Carla's shirt _____   Rob's shirt _____

Listen

8 (1 24) Listen. In your notebook, list three things that are important to Astrid.

Write

9 On a piece of paper, write a paragraph about people and things that are important to you.

 Extra practice
• Student Book, page 113, Lesson 2B
• Language Builder: WB, page 12; GB, page 103
• Student CD-ROM, Unit 2

Grammar	How much is . . .
	How much are . . .
Vocabulary	Fast food
Function	Order food and drinks
	Use *can* to request something

Get started

1 What's your favorite fast food?

Vocabulary: Fast food

2 🔊 ₂₅ Look at the menu. Listen and point to the food and drinks you hear. Which words are not in the pictures?

Joe's Café

Menu

Food/Snacks

Burger	$3.75
Hot dog	$1.75
Chicken sandwich	$5.50
Cheese sandwich	$5.50
Potato chips	75¢
Ice cream	$2.00

Drinks

Soda	75¢
Bottled water	$1.00
Orange juice	$1.50
Milk	$1.00
Tea	$1.00
Coffee	$1.50
Hot chocolate	$1.75

Presentation

3 🔊 ₂₆ Listen and read along. Circle the prices.

Carlos: Hello. **How much are** the sandwiches?

Joe: Chicken or cheese?

Carlos: Cheese.

Joe: They're $5.50.

Carlos: OK! **Can I have** a cheese sandwich and hot chocolate, **please**?

Joe: Here you go.

Carlos: Thanks. **How much is** that?

Joe: That's $7.25, please. Thank you. Next, please.

Polly: **Can I have** a bag of potato chips, a bottle of water, two hot dogs, and ice cream **please**?

Carlos: Polly! You're kidding!

Polly: You know me. I'm always hungry!

Comprehension

4 What do Carlos and Polly order?

	Food	Drink
Carlos	*cheese sandwich*	
Polly		

Solve it!

5 Look at the menu and the conversation. How much is Polly's food and drink?

Joe's Café

American money

Bills: $1, $5, $10, $20, $50, $100
Coins: 1¢, 5¢, 10¢, 25¢

- 50¢ = fifty cents
- $1 = one dollar
- $2.50 = two dollars and fifty cents
- $5 = five dollars

Practice

6 🎧 (1/27) Listen and write the amounts you hear.

a) _____$35_____ b) _____
c) _____ d) _____
e) _____ f) _____

Grammar

How much is/How much are

Question	Answer
How much is a burger?	It's $3.75.
How much is a can of soda?	It's 75 cents.
How much are the sandwiches?	They're $5.50 each.

☞ Go to page 129, Master your grammar.

Practice

7 PAIRS Choose three items from the menu on page 16. Ask your partner about the prices. Take turns asking and answering questions.

A: *How much is/are ... ?*
B: *It's/They're ...*

Use your English: Order food and drinks

8 🎧 (1/28) **GROUPS** Listen again to the conversation in Exercise 3.

Customer	Server
Ask for food and drink	**Check**
• Can I have a sandwich, please?	• Chicken or cheese?
• Can I have two hot dogs, please?	• Here you go. Anything else?
Ask the price	**Say the price**
• How much is a bag of chips?	• It's 75¢.
• How much are the sandwiches?	• They're $5.50.
• How much is that altogether?	• It's $6.25.

9 GROUPS Roleplay a conversation similar to the one in Exercise 3. Use the menu in Exercise 2.

Write

10 PAIRS Pretend you have a fast-food restaurant. First discuss your plans for the restaurant's menu. Then write a menu for your restaurant on a piece of paper. Include the price for each item.

A: *Let's plan our menu. For food, we can sell hot dogs, ...*
B: *Yes. So how much is ... ?*

> ### Extra practice
> - **Student Book, page 114, Lesson 2C**
> - **Language Builder: WB page 14; GB, page 104**
> - **Student CD-ROM, Unit 2**

CONSOLIDATION

INTEGRATED SKILLS

Values for living

Get started

1 Which of the items below would you give to family and friends? Look at the photos below and match each present to a person.

___ your mother ___ your brother ___ a friend
___ a girl or boy you like ___ your sister

The necklace is a good present for my ...

1 a necklace

2 a computer game

3 flowers

4 sneakers

5 a CD

6 chocolate

Read

2 🎧 1/29 Listen and read the conversations. When is Alex's mother's birthday?

Comprehension

3 Read the conversations again and write *T* for *true* or *F* for *false*. Underline the false information.

_____ 1 The sneakers are Brad's birthday present.
_____ 2 Brad's sneakers are black and white.
_____ 3 Plain white is Alex's favorite color.
_____ 4 The sneakers are $80.

💡 Solve it!

4 How much is Alex's allowance each week?

1

Alex: Hey, Brad! Those are really great sneakers!
Brad: Thanks. They're a birthday present from my Mom and Dad.
Alex: They're really cool. My sneakers are awful! I need a new pair.

2

Stella: Look. Those are the same as Brad's sneakers. What are your favorite colors? Black and white or plain white?
Alex: Black and white. Which ones do you like?

3

Alex: Mom, can I borrow $90 for new sneakers?
Mom: $90 for sneakers! That's expensive.
Alex: I know, but they're really cool. Please, Mom! You can take it out of my allowance.
Mom: Oh, all right. Here you go. But no allowance for six weeks, OK?
Alex: OK. Thanks, Mom. You rock!

4

Alex: See you later, Dad.
Dad: Where are you going?
Alex: I'm going to the mall to buy new sneakers.
Dad: OK, but don't forget, your mother's birthday is next week.
Alex: Oh, no!

New words
- birthday • the same as • plain (white)
- borrow • expensive • really
- allowance • don't forget . . .

Listen

Learning strategy: Listen a second time
When you listen for the first time, you won't understand everything. Don't worry! Listen again. The next time you listen, you will understand more.

5 🎧 1/30 Listen to Alex and complete the chart.

Price	Item
	necklace
$20.00	
$15.00	
	black-and-white sneakers
	plain white sneakers

Speak your mind!

Speaking tip: Be willing to make mistakes
When you speak, don't worry about making mistakes. Just keep talking!

6 What's the best idea? What's your suggestion for Alex? Give your opinion.
- Buy the black-and-white sneakers.
- Buy the chocolate, the flowers, and the sneakers.
- Buy the necklace and the plain white sneakers.
- Give his mom another present. (What?)
  I think it's OK to . . .

Listen

7 🎧 1/31 Listen. What does Alex buy for his mother?

Write

8 In your notebook, make a list of birthday presents for your mom. On another piece of paper, choose the one that you think is the best and describe it.

A necklace is a good present for my mom. It's black and brown . . . It costs . . .

CLIL PROJECT, page 140

19

Grammar (40 points)

1 Complete the conversation with the correct form of the verb *be*. (9 points)

Alex: Hi, Julia. How ⁰ ___are___ you?

Julia: Fine, thanks. And you?

Alex: OK, thanks. What ¹ _____ that?

Julia: It ² _____ a photo of Keira.

Alex: ³ _____ Keira your friend?

Julia: No, she ⁴ _____. She ⁵ _____ my sister. She ⁶ _____ in Canada right now.

Alex: ⁷ _____ you and your sister Canadian?

Julia: No, we ⁸ _____, but our grandparents ⁹ _____ from Canada.

2 Complete the sentences with *my, your, his, her, its, our,* or *their*. (6 points)

0 Hello. What's ___your___ name?

1 I'm from the U.S., but _____ father is from Peru.

2 The boys are brothers. _____ parents are Spanish.

3 Where's Maria? _____ keys are on the table.

4 David is my friend. _____ family is from France.

5 It's a nice dog! What's _____ name?

6 I'm Paul and this is my brother, Chris. _____ last name is White.

3 Write sentences with the correct form of *be* and the possessive (singular *'s* or plural *s'*). (6 points)

0 It/Gary/bike *It's Gary's bike.*

00 They/my/friends/backpacks
They're my friends' backpacks.

1 She/Rafael/mother

_____

2 It/my parents/dog

_____

3 They/Sarah/brothers

_____

4 He/Bernard/father

_____

5 Those/the girls/notebooks

_____

6 These/Justin/keys

4 Write questions and answers about the pictures. Use the correct form of the words in the box. (10 points)

> • sneaker • ~~bike~~ • key • ~~cell phone~~
> • ID card • hat • sandwich

0 What's this?
  It's a cell phone.

00 What are those?
  They're bikes.

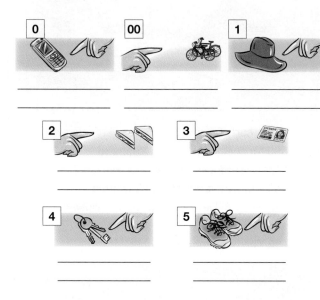

| 0 | 00 | 1 |

_____ _____ _____

_____ _____ _____

| 2 | 3 |

_____ _____

_____ _____

| 4 | 5 |

_____ _____

_____ _____

5 Circle the correct words to complete the article. (9 points)

NEW STUDENT at Seattle Central Middle School

by Kevin Yang

Fernando Martinez ⁰ (is)/are a new student at our school. He ¹ is/am 13 years old. He ² is/are from Colombia. His parents ³ are/is from Colombia also. He has two sisters. ⁴ Their/They're names ⁵ are/am Isabelle and Lidia. ⁶ They're/Their eight and eleven years old.

What are Fernando's favorites?
⁷ My /I'm favorite bands ⁸ are/is Coldplay and Linkin Park. ⁹ My/I'm favorite movie is *Avatar*. Welcome to our school, Fernando!

Vocabulary (40 points)

6 Write the missing numbers. (5 points)

0 thirty forty _fifty_ sixty

1 ten eleven _____ thirteen

2 four six _____ ten

3 twenty-three twenty-five _____
twenty-nine

4 twenty-two thirty-three _____ fifty-five

5 ninety-seven ninety-eight ninety-nine

_____

7 Complete the sentences with a country from the box and a nationality. (14 points)

> • Mexico • Spain • the U.K. • Japan
> • ~~Brazil~~ • Italy • Colombia • the U.S.

0 Miguel is from São Paulo, _Brazil_. He's _Brazilian_.

1 Mika is from Tokyo, _____ . She's _____ .

2 Tom is from New York, _____ . He's _____ .

3 José is from Mexico City, _____ . He's _____ .

4 Carina is from Rome, _____ . She's _____ .

5 Nicole is from London, _____ . She's _____ .

6 Pedro is from Bogotá, _____ . He's _____ .

7 Emilia is from Madrid, _____ . She's _____ .

8 What color are the T-shirts? (7 points)

9 Write sentences in your notebook. Name the food or drink and the price. (14 points)

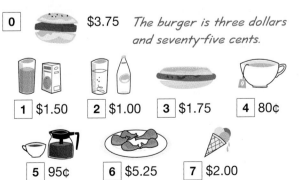

0 $3.75 _The burger is three dollars and seventy-five cents._

1 $1.50 2 $1.00 3 $1.75 4 80¢

5 95¢ 6 $5.25 7 $2.00

Use your English (20 points)

10 Complete each conversation with an expression from the box. (10 points)

> • Thanks! • Nice to meet you. • I don't know.
> • ~~Yuck!~~ • Don't be silly! • How are you?

0 A: This is a chicken and chocolate sandwich.
  B: _____ _Yuck!_ _____

1 A: This is my friend, Sally.
  B: _____

2 A: This hot dog is $10!
  B: _____

3 A: Where is Bruno from?
  B: _____

4 A: Your cell phone is really cool.
  B: _____

5 A: Hello, Ben. _____
  B: Fine, thanks.

11 Number the lines in the correct order to make a conversation.

Conversation 1 (5 points)

_____ a) Me? I'm fine, thanks.

_1_ b) Hi, Beth! How are things?

_____ c) Good-bye.

_____ d) Not bad, thanks, Adrian. How are you?

_____ e) Yes, see you on Friday, Beth. Bye.

_____ f) See you on Friday?

Conversation 2 (5 points)

_____ a) They're $5.50 each.

_____ b) That's $7.00, please.

_____ c) Sure. Anything else?

_1_ d) How much are the chicken sandwiches?

_____ e) Can I have a chicken sandwich and
orange juice, please?

_____ f) No, thanks. How much is that?

SELF-CHECK	
Grammar	_____ /40
Vocabulary	_____ /40
Use your English	_____ /20
Total score	_____ /100

Homes

3

There's no bathtub.

Grammar	*There is*: affirmative, negative, and *yes/no* questions
	Definite article: *the*
Vocabulary	Rooms, parts of a house, fixtures, and appliances
Function	Talk about your dream house

Get started

1 GROUPS Discuss: Would you like to live in a really big house or a really small one? Explain your answer.

Read

2 Listen and read along. Why is Jay Shafer's house different?

The Smallest House
in the World

This is Jay Shafer and this is his house. It's made of wood. It's very, very small. It's the smallest house in the world!

Downstairs there's a living room, a kitchen, and a bathroom. Is there a bathtub? No, there isn't, but there's a shower and a toilet. The kitchen is very small. There's a stove, a refrigerator, and a sink, but there's no dishwasher—unfortunately! There's a small desk in the living room. There isn't a dining room, but there's a table. It folds up under the desk. There's a front porch, too.

Upstairs there's a small bedroom. The house is 96 square feet. That's the size of some people's bathrooms!

The house even has wheels so you can move it around. Pretty cool!

Comprehension

3a Do the following:

1 In the article above, underline the names of the rooms in Jay Shafer's house.
2 Circle the names of the fixtures and appliances.

b Say one more thing that is unique in Jay's house.

It is only 96 square feet.

💡 Solve it!

4 What two rooms are missing from Jay Shafer's house?

Vocabulary: Rooms, parts of a house, fixtures, and appliances

5a 🎧 1/33 Listen and repeat.

Rooms
- bathroom • bedroom • dining room
- kitchen • living room • porch • garage

Parts of a house
- door • downstairs • floor • upstairs
- wall • window • yard

Fixtures and appliances
- bathtub • dishwasher • refrigerator
- shower • sink • stove • toilet
- washing machine

b Label the appliances and fixtures on the right. Where do they belong?

The dishwasher belongs in the kitchen.

Grammar

There is/There isn't (There's no)	
Affirmative	**Negative**
There's a bathroom.	There's no bathtub. OR There isn't a bathtub.
Questions	**Short answers**
Is there a bathtub?	Yes, there is./No, there isn't.

Definite article: *the*

Downstairs there's a dining room and a kitchen. The kitchen is very small.

☞ Go to page 130, Master your grammar.

Practice

6a Complete these sentences about Jay's house. Use *There is, There isn't*, or *There's no*.

1 ___*There's*___ a red door.
2 _____ bathtub.
3 _____ a window upstairs.
4 _____ a porch.
5 _____ garage.

b PAIRS Ask *yes/no* questions about the sentences in Exercise 6a.

A: *Is there a red door?* B: *Yes, there is.*

7 Which of these appliances and fixtures are in your kitchen and bathroom? Write sentences in your notebook.

There's a ... / There's no ...

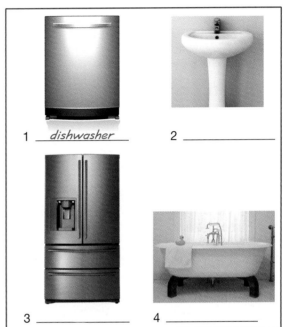

1 ___*dishwasher*___   2 _____

3 _____   4 _____

Pronunciation: /ð/ there

8 🎧 Go to page 126.

Listen

9 🎧 1/36 Listen to the Audio. Write two more things you hear about the room.

1 *It's very small.*   3 _____

2 _____

Speak

10 PAIRS Talk about your dream house. Use these questions to help you with ideas.
- Is it big or small? • What rooms does it have?
- What appliances and fixtures are/aren't there?

Write

11 Draw or find pictures of your dream house. Write a description of it on a piece of paper. Use your information from Exercise 10.

My dream house is really cool! There's a ...

> **Extra practice**
- Student Book, page 114, Lesson 3A
- Language Builder: WB page 18; GB, page 106
- Student CD-ROM, Unit 3

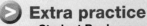

23

3B Are there any DVDs?

Grammar	*There are*: affirmative, negative, and *yes/no* questions *Some* and *any* with plural nouns
Vocabulary	Furniture
Function	Talk about a student lounge

Get started

1 Look at the pictures on the right. Point to the ones you have in your home.

Vocabulary: Furniture

2a 🎧 (1/37) Now listen and repeat. Label the pictures on the right with words from the box.

- armchair • bed • bookcase • cabinet
- CD player • chair • clock • computer
- desk • dresser • DVD player • lamp • mirror
- shelf • sofa • table • television (TV)
- wardrobe • wastebasket

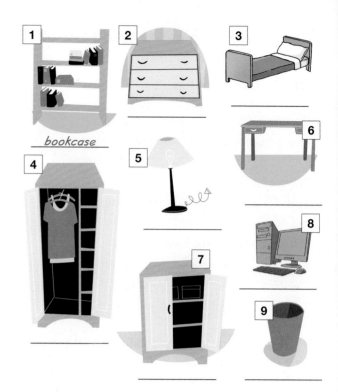

bookcase

b Look at the photo below. Label the objects with words from Exercise 2a.

Presentation

3 🎧 (1/38) Listen and read along. Circle the furniture words.

Zach: OK, guys, this is the new club room. **There aren't any** computers yet, but **there are some** chairs, **an** armchair, and a sofa. What do you think?

David: It's great, Zach! There's a TV and a DVD player, too.

Laura: Yeah! It's really cool. **Are there any** DVDs?

Zach: No, **there aren't**. Not yet. Sorry, guys.

Polly: This is a nice bookcase, but where are the books?

Zach: Ah, **there aren't any** books yet.

Carlos: Is there a CD player?

Zach: Yes, there is. **And there are some** CDs on the table.

Carlos: Let's see. Oh! Hits of the 80s. That's not really my kind of music.

clock

24

Phrases

🎧 1/39 Listen and repeat.

- Let's see. • Sorry,
- not really my kind of [music].
- What do you think?

Comprehension

4 Check (✓) the objects that are in the new club room.

☐ a sofa ☐ armchair
☐ a bookcase ☐ DVDs
☐ books ☐ a DVD player
☐ computers ☐ CDs
☐ CD player ☐ a TV

💡 Solve it!

5 Find six words from Exercise 2a that are not in the photo.

Grammar

There are/There aren't

Affirmative	Negative
There are some chairs.	**There aren't** any desks.
Questions	**Short answers**
Are there any DVDs?	Yes, **there are.**/No, **there aren't.**

Some and any

Affirmative	Negative
There are **some** CDs.	There aren't **any** computers.
Questions	
Are there **any** DVDs?	Yes, **there are.**/No, **there aren't.**

☞ Go to page 130, Master your grammar.

Practice

6 In your notebook, write sentences using *there are*, *there aren't*, and *some* or *any*.

1 desks/in this classroom / ✓
   There are some desks in this classroom.
2 chairs/in the club room / **?**
   Are there any chairs in the club room?
3 computers/in this school / **?**
4 sofas/in that coffee shop / ✗
5 books/in that cabinet / ✓
6 good DVDs/in that store / **?**
7 CDs/on the shelf / ✗
8 chairs/over there / ✓

7 In your notebook, write two more sentences comparing Zach's club room and your classroom.
There aren't any desks in the club room, but there are some desks in this classroom.

Speak

8 GROUPS Plan a student lounge where students can meet and relax. Use *There are*, *There aren't*, and *Are there*.

Write

9 GROUPS On a piece of paper, write a description of your proposed student lounge. Use your notes from Exercise 8. Share your plans with another group.

> **Extra practice**
> • Student Book, page 114, Lesson 3B
> • Language Builder: WB, page 20; GB, page 106
> • Student CD-ROM, Unit 3

It's on the floor.

Get started

1 Study the photo carefully. Then close your book. What can you remember?

There's a table.

Presentation

2  Listen and read along. Where is David's MP3 player?

Laura:	David, can I borrow your cell phone?
David:	Sure. It's **on** the table.
Laura:	Thanks. Whoa! Your room's really messy! Oh, can I borrow your MP3 player, too?
David:	Sorry, Laura, I need it.
Laura:	Please, David! Just for tonight?
David:	All right. It's **in** my backpack.
Laura:	Thanks! Where's your backpack?
David:	It's here, **next to** my chair.
Laura:	Your MP3 player isn't **in** your backpack. It's here **on** the floor, **under** the table.
Carlos:	This is a cool game! Can I borrow it?
David:	Oh, no! Not you, too.

Comprehension

3 Answer the questions.

1 What two things does Laura want to borrow?
2 What does Carlos want to borrow?
3 Whose bedroom is messy?

Grammar

Prepositions of place

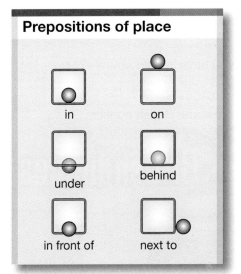

in   on

under   behind

in front of   next to

☞ Go to page 130, Master your grammar.

Practice

4 **PAIRS** Ask and answer questions about the people and objects in David's bedroom.

1 cell phone (table)
   A: *Where's the cell phone?*
   B: *It's on the table.*
2 television (window)
3 Laura (Carlos)
4 MP3 player (floor)
5 backpack (chair)
6 book (bed)

5 **PAIRS** Student A, study the photo on page 26. Then close your book. Student B, ask Student A where these objects are.
B: *Where's the backpack?*
A: *It's on the floor.*

1 magazines   3 model car
2 soccer ball   4 pictures

Solve it!

6 (1/41) Look at the picture at the top of the right column as you listen. There are five mistakes on the audio. What are they?

1 The sofa isn't behind the cabinet. It's next to the cabinet.

Use your English: Make and respond to requests

7 (1/42) **PAIRS** Listen and repeat. Then practice the conversation.

A: Can I borrow your pen?
B: Sure. Here you go.
A: Thanks. Can I borrow your MP3 player, too?
B: No, I'm sorry. I need it.

Make a request
• Can I borrow . . .?
Agree
• Yes, OK. • Yes, of course. • Sure.
Refuse
• No, I'm sorry. I need it. • Sorry. I'm using it.

8 **PAIRS** Practice more conversations. Use these words: book, CD, cell phone, DVD, magazine.

Write

9 On a piece of paper, describe your bedroom and say where things are.

In my bedroom there's a bed. There's a chair next to the bed. . . .

 Extra practice
• Student Book, page 115, Lesson 3C
• Language Builder: WB, page 23; GB, page 107
• Student CD-ROM, Unit 3

3c

27

INTEGRATED CONSOLIDATION SKILLS

Across cultures

Get started

1 Look at the photos of houses below. Which types of houses do you have in your country?

Read

2 Read the factfiles about American and British homes. How old are some British houses?

American homes

British homes

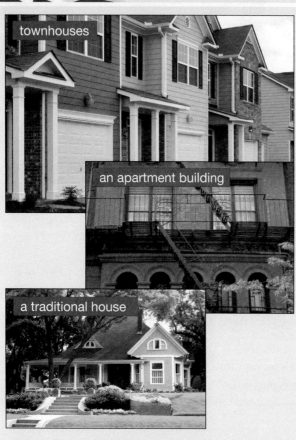

townhouses

an apartment building

a traditional house

a detached house

semi-detached houses

terraced houses

U.S. Factfile

- There are about 100 million homes in the U.S. Some are apartments, but most are houses.
- Old houses in the U.S. are about 200 years old. There aren't many old houses.
- Sixty-eight percent of American families live in a house. Twenty-five percent live in an apartment.
- The average American home has three televisions.
- There's a pet in 60% of American homes.

U.K. Factfile

- There are about 22 million homes in the U.K. Some are apartments, but most are houses.
- There are many old British houses. Some are 500 years old.
- Eighty percent of British families live in a house. Only 15% live in apartments.
- There are four televisions in the average British home.
- There's a pet in 52% of British homes.

Comprehension

3 Write *U.S.* or *U.K.* next to each sentence.

1 There are about 100 million houses. _____

2 Some houses are 500 years old. _____

3 The average household has four TV sets. _____

4 Sixty percent of the homes have pets. _____

> **Learning strategy: Visualize or create a mental picture**
>
> In order to understand a descriptive paragraph, visualize or draw the images described.

4a Read about Daniela and draw a sketch of her bedroom.

Daniela from Baltimore talks about her house.

"I live with my mother, father, and sister in a townhouse. Our townhouse is small, but it's nice. There are two bedrooms and a bathroom upstairs. Downstairs there's a living room, a dining room, a kitchen, and a small bathroom. There's one TV in the living room and one in my mom and dad's room. There's a big backyard and a garden. My sister and I share a bedroom. There are two beds and a dresser for our clothes. I'm not very neat, but my sister is. I drive her crazy because I'm so messy."

> **New words**
> • backyard • clothes • drive . . . crazy • garden
> • messy • neat

b Complete column 1 in the chart.

	Daniela	Gerry
Type of house	*townhouse*	
Number of bedrooms		
Total number of rooms		
Number of TV sets		
Outside		

Listen

5 🔊 1/43 Listen to the conversation. Complete column 2 in the chart in Exercise 4b.

Speak

6 PAIRS Talk about your home. Answer the questions.

• Is it a house or an apartment?

• How many bedrooms are there?

• Is there a yard/garden?

• What's your favorite room or place in the house?

Write

> **Writing tip: Punctuation**
>
> Use punctuation to make your writing clear.
>
> • Use a **period** at the end of a sentence. Start a new sentence with a **capital letter**.
> *Upstairs there are three bedrooms and a bathroom. There isn't a porch.*
>
> • Use a **comma** to combine a list of three or more things.
> *There's a living room, a dining room, and a kitchen on the first floor.*
>
> • Use a **question mark** at the end of a question.
> *How many bedrooms are there?*
>
> • Use an **exclamation mark** at the end of surprising or funny sentences.
> *All my things are on the floor!*

7 Correct these sentences. Use capital letters and the correct punctuation.

1 our apartment is really big there are three bedrooms

_____

2 there's a television in the bathroom

_____

3 where's your house

_____

4 there's a swimming pool a big yard and a garage

_____

8 Write a paragraph about your home. Use Daniela's text in Exercise 4a as a model. Remember to use the correct punctuation.

I live with my . . . in a . . . .

CLIL PROJECT, page 140

Grammar *Have* with *I, you, we, they*
Vocabulary Family
Function Talk about your family

Get started

1 Do you go to the circus? Do you like going there? What do you like about it?

Read

2 ₄₄¹ Listen and read along. Circle the family words.

My family

A FAMILY BUSINESS

Ben Crawford's family is different from other families. All the family members are trapeze artists in Circus Zazel. "Circus Zazel is a family business," says 15-year-old Ben. "I **have** one brother and one sister. My brother's name is George, and my sister's name is Francesca. We're all trapeze artists like my mom, Jill, and my dad, Harry. My dad's parents—my grandparents— Nancy and Fred, are now retired. They were the circus clowns!"

Ben, George, and Francesca also **have** an aunt, uncle, and a cousin who work in Circus Zazel. "Aunt Jane and her husband, Rob, are jugglers. Their son, Alan, is an acrobat. Alan is an only child," says Ben.

Do Ben, his brother, sister, and cousin go to school? Yes, they do. Ben's mother is their teacher. They **have** lessons every morning in their caravan. What about school friends? "I **don't have** any school friends," says Ben, "but I **have** a lot of circus friends, and that's cool."

A juggler

Acrobats

Trapeze artists

Note
Jill and Harry are Ben's **parents**.
His grandmother and grandfather are his **grandparents**.
Alan is an **only child**.

Comprehension

3a Write each person's job.

1 Ben _____ 5 Alan _____

2 Rob _____ 6 George _____

3 Francesca _____ 7 Jane _____

4 Jill _____ 8 Harry _____

b Complete the Crawford family tree.

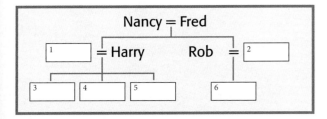

Vocabulary: Family

4 🎧 (1/45) Complete the chart with family words from the text. Then listen, check, and repeat.

Male	Female
grandfather	grandmother
father (dad)	4
1	sister
2	daughter
3	wife
uncle	5
nephew	niece
cousin	cousin

5 PAIRS Ask and answer questions about three members of the Crawford family.

A: *Who is Ben?*   B: *George's brother.*

Grammar

Have with *I, you, we, they*	
Affirmative	**Negative**
I **have** a brother.	I **don't have** any sisters.
Questions	**Short answers**
Do you **have** a brother?	Yes, I **do**. No, I **don't**.
> How many cousins **do** you **have**? Five.	

☞ Go to page 131, Master your grammar.

Practice

6a Complete the interview with Francesca with the correct form of the verb *have*.

Q: ¹ _____*Do*_____ you ² _____*have*_____ a big family?

F: No, I ³ _____ . I ⁴_____ a small family.

Q: Really? How many brothers and sisters ⁵ _____ you ⁶ _____?

F: I ⁷ _____ two brothers, but I ⁸ _____ any sisters.

Q: ⁹ _____ you and your brother ¹⁰ _____ any pets?

F: No, we ¹¹ _____ . No, wait. We ¹² _____ any cats or dogs, but we ¹³ _____ a goldfish!

Q: ¹⁴ _____ you ¹⁵ _____ a boyfriend?

F: No, I ¹⁶ _____ . I ¹⁷ _____ time for a boyfriend. I'm a full-time trapeze artist!

b PAIRS Interview your partner about his or her family. Use the questions in Exercise 6a.

Use your English: Talk about your family

7 🎧 (1/46) PAIRS Listen and repeat. Then practice the conversation.

A: Do you have any brothers or sisters?

B: Yes, I do. I have two brothers and a sister.

A: How old are they?

B: My brothers are 11 and 18, and my sister's five.

A: How many cousins do you have?

B: I have ten cousins.

Write

8 On a piece of paper, write about your family. Use the questions in Exercises 6 and 7 for ideas.

I have a really big family. I . . . brothers and . . . sisters. . . .

 Extra practice
- **Student Book, page 115, Lesson 4A**
- **Language Builder: WB, page 26; GB, page 109**
- **Student CD-ROM, Unit 4**

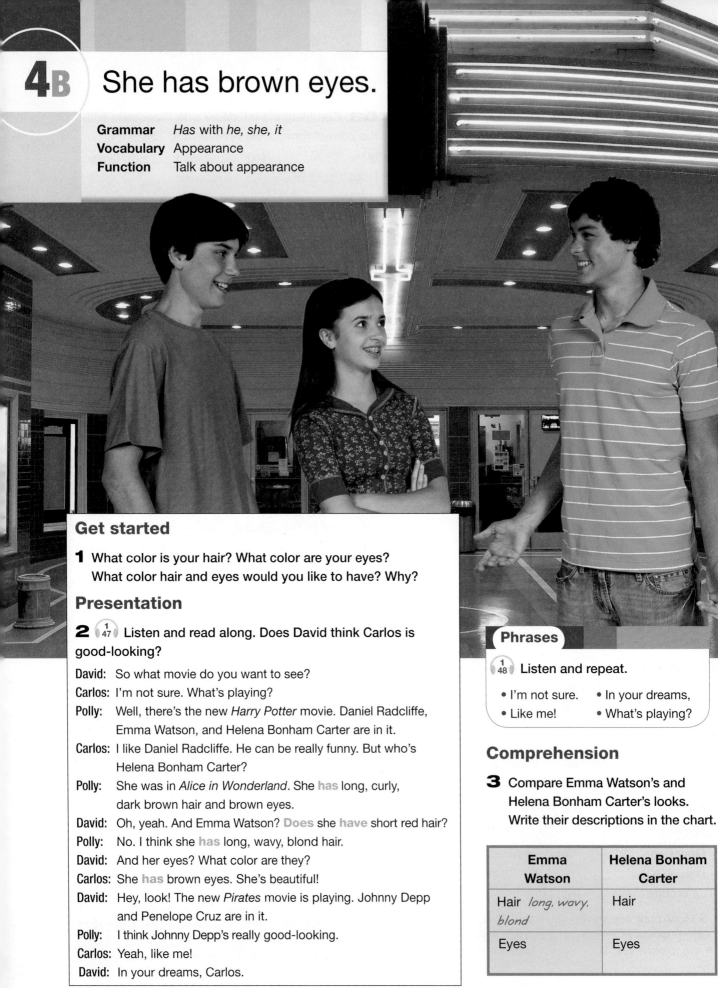

4B She has brown eyes.

Grammar *Has* with *he, she, it*
Vocabulary Appearance
Function Talk about appearance

Get started

1 What color is your hair? What color are your eyes?
What color hair and eyes would you like to have? Why?

Presentation

2 🎧 1/47 Listen and read along. Does David think Carlos is good-looking?

David: So what movie do you want to see?

Carlos: I'm not sure. What's playing?

Polly: Well, there's the new *Harry Potter* movie. Daniel Radcliffe, Emma Watson, and Helena Bonham Carter are in it.

Carlos: I like Daniel Radcliffe. He can be really funny. But who's Helena Bonham Carter?

Polly: She was in *Alice in Wonderland*. She **has** long, curly, dark brown hair and brown eyes.

David: Oh, yeah. And Emma Watson? **Does** she **have** short red hair?

Polly: No. I think she **has** long, wavy, blond hair.

David: And her eyes? What color are they?

Carlos: She **has** brown eyes. She's beautiful!

David: Hey, look! The new *Pirates* movie is playing. Johnny Depp and Penelope Cruz are in it.

Polly: I think Johnny Depp's really good-looking.

Carlos: Yeah, like me!

David: In your dreams, Carlos.

Phrases

🎧 1/48 Listen and repeat.

- I'm not sure.
- Like me!
- In your dreams,
- What's playing?

Comprehension

3 Compare Emma Watson's and Helena Bonham Carter's looks. Write their descriptions in the chart.

Emma Watson	Helena Bonham Carter
Hair *long, wavy, blond*	Hair
Eyes	Eyes

Vocabulary: Appearance

4a 🔊 ¹⁄₄₉ Listen and repeat.

Hair style
- short • long • medium-length • straight
- wavy • curly

Hair color
- black • dark • dark brown • brown • red
- light brown • gray • fair • blond • white

Eye color
- brown • blue • green • hazel

Other features
- a moustache • a beard • eyeglasses

Other adjectives
- young • old • middle-aged • tall • short
- medium-height • beautiful • good-looking

b Use some words from Exercise 4a for each celebrity.

Penelope Cruz *brown eyes,* _____

Johnny Depp _____

Penelope Cruz   Johnny Depp

Grammar

Has with he, she, it	
Affirmative	**Negative**
She **has** brown eyes.	She **doesn't have** blue eyes.
Questions	**Short answers**
Does she **have** brown eyes?	Yes, she **does**. No, she **doesn't**.

☞ Go to page 131, Master your grammar.

Practice

5 Complete the description of Diego Luna. Then write descriptions of Shia LaBeouf and Amanda Seyfried in your notebook.

Diego Luna _____ medium-length, brown hair. He _____ brown eyes. He _____ a moustache or a beard. He's medium-height.

Name: Diego Luna
Brown eyes; no moustache; medium-height

Name: Shia LaBeouf
Hazel eyes; beard and moustache; medium-height

Name: Amanda Seyfried
Green eyes; long hair; short

Speak

6 GROUPS Think of someone in your class. The other members must ask questions and guess who the person is.

- Is it a man/woman/boy/girl?
- What kind of hair does he or she have?
- What color eyes does he or she have?

Write

7 On a piece of paper, write a description of your favorite actor or actress.

My favorite actor is ... He has blue eyes ...

> **Extra practice**
> - **Student Book, page 115, Lesson 4B**
> - **Language Builder: WB, page 28; GB, page 110**
> - **Student CD-ROM, Unit 4**

4c When's your birthday?

Grammar	Prepositions of time: *in, on*
Vocabulary	Months and seasons
	Ordinal numbers
Function	Talk about important dates

Get started

1 GROUPS When is your birthday? Identify the oldest and youngest student in your group.

Vocabulary: Months and seasons

2a 🎧 1/50 Write the months in the chart in the correct order. Then listen and repeat.

Months
- October • January • March • December
- May • July • April • September
- February • June • August • November

Seasons
- spring • summer • fall • winter

January			

b Write the start of each season under the appropriate month in the chart in Exercise 2a.

Vocabulary: Ordinal numbers

3 🎧 1/51 Listen and repeat.

1st first	8th eighth	15th fifteenth
2nd second	9th ninth	20th twentieth
3rd third	10th tenth	21st twenty-first
4th fourth	11th eleventh	30th thirtieth
5th fifth	12th twelfth	31st thirty-first
6th sixth	13th thirteenth	
7th seventh	14th fourteenth	

Note

When writing dates, use cardinal numbers, but when speaking, use ordinal numbers.

4 PAIRS Student A says three numbers from 1 to 31. Student B says the ordinal numbers.

A: *three, seven, twenty-one*

B: *third, seventh, twenty-first*

5a PAIRS Choose a month. Write it and the year at the top of the calendar below. In the boxes, write the dates (1–28, 30, or 31). Then note important events such as tests, homework, birthdays, etc.

b GROUPS Join with another pair and take turns talking about the information in your calendars from Exercise 5a.

September third is my birthday. The fifth is the day we pick up my new dog!

Pronunciation: /θ/ <u>th</u>ree

6 🎧 Go to page 126.

Sunday	Monday	Tuesday	Wednesday	Thursday	Friday	Saturday

Presentation

7 Listen and read along. In which month is Polly's birthday? Laura's birthday?

Laura: Hey, let's read this month's horoscope.

Polly: I don't really believe in horoscopes, but OK. Just for fun.

Laura: When's your birthday?

Polly: It's **on** July 17.

Laura: What's your sign?

Polly: You mean my zodiac sign? It's Cancer.

Laura: You're lucky. Your birthday is **in** the summer. Mine is **in** December—**on** New Year's Eve.

Polly: So you're a Capricorn. OK. What does my horoscope say?

Laura: Be prepared for a difficult week.

Polly: Nah, I don't believe it. I'm having an easy week. Wait a minute . . . I have a math test this week, an English test, a geography test . . .

Laura: That's a lot of tests. When are they?

Polly: Well, math is **on** Friday, English is **on** Wednesday, and geography is **on** Thursday! Oh, no! My horoscope is right!

💡 Solve it!

8 What's the exact date of Laura's birthday?

Comprehension

9 Write *Polly* or *Laura*.

1 She doesn't believe in horoscopes. ___*Polly*___
2 Her sign is Cancer. _____
3 Her birthday is on New Year's Eve. _____
4 Her sign is Capricorn. _____
5 Her birthday is in the summer. _____
6 She has a lot of tests. _____

Grammar

Prepositions of time: *in, on*	
Question	**Answer**
When's your birthday?	It's **in** July. (Month) It's **in** the summer. (Season) It's **on** July 17. (Date) It's **on** Monday. (Day)

☞ Go to page 131, Master your grammar.

Practice

10 Look at Polly's notes. Answer these questions in complete sentences in your notebook.

When is . . .
1 Polly's English test?
2 her math test?
3 the field trip?
4 the last day of school?
5 Laura's birthday?

Important dates

English test = Wednesday
Geography test = Thursday
Math test = Friday
Field trip = spring
Last day of school = June 19
Laura's birthday =
New Year's Eve

Speak

11a PAIRS Ask and answer questions about your birthday and your zodiac sign.
A: *When's your birthday?*   A: *What's your sign?*
B: *It's on April 23.*   B: *It's Taurus.*

b PAIRS Ask questions about important school dates.

Write

12 In your notebook, write notes about this month's school events (for example, tests). Compare your notes with another student's.

 Extra practice
• **Student Book, page 116, Lesson 4C**
• **Language Builder: WB, page 30; GB, page 110**
• **Student CD-ROM, Unit 4**

Curriculum link: Science

Get started

1 Do you know any twins? Can you tell them apart? How?

Read

2 Read the article. What is the name for twins who look exactly the same?

> **Learning strategy: Guess the meaning of new words**
>
> When you read, don't stop when you see a new or difficult word. Try to guess its meaning from the words and phrases near that word. If you still don't know the meaning of the word, use a dictionary.

Twins   The same but different

by Science reporter David Smith

There are more than six billion people in the world, but no one looks exactly like you— unless you are a twin. Brothers and sisters are different, but identical twins look the same. Why is this? The answer is in our genes.

What are genes?

Genes are pieces of biological information from our parents. Fifty percent of our genes are from our mother, and fifty percent come from our father.

Why are brothers and sisters different?

They are different because each person takes different genes from his or her parents.

Why do identical twins look the same?

They look the same because they have the same genes.

Are identical twins exactly the same?

No, identical twins aren't exactly the same. Their personalities and their fingerprints are different.

Are all twins identical?

No, not all twins are identical. Twins who are not identical are called fraternal twins. Fraternal twins have the same birthday, of course!

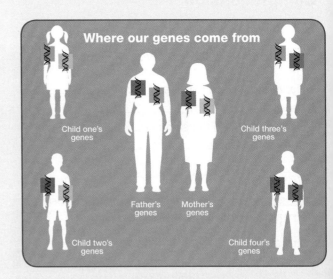

Where our genes come from

Child one's genes · Child three's genes · Father's genes · Mother's genes · Child two's genes · Child four's genes

> **New words**
> - billion • biological • exactly • fingerprints
> - fraternal • genes • identical • information
> - no one • of course • personality(ies) • piece
> - soccer team • truth • twins • unless • way

36

Comprehension

3 Circle the correct answer.

1 We get _____ our genes from our parents.
   a) half b) all
2 Identical twins have _____ genes.
   a) the same b) different
3 Identical twins have _____ personalities and fingerprints.
   a) the same b) different
4 James and Oliver Phelps are _____ twins.
   a) identical b) fraternal
5 James and Oliver's favorites are _____.
   a) the same b) different

The Phelps twins

James and Oliver Phelps are British actors. They played the roles of Fred and George Weasley, respectively, in the *Harry Potter* movies. James and Oliver are identical twins. They have the same hairstyle and hair color, the same eye color, and the same height. Both like the Red Hot Chili Peppers, the Foo Fighters, and Coldplay. But they are different in many ways. They support different soccer teams, and they like different food. They also have different tastes in movies. Oliver's favorite movie is *Avatar*, while James's favorite is *District 9*. But are they good friends? Of course, they are.

Listen

4a 🎧 1/55 Listen. Which is Kelly and which is Joanna?

Kelly has

_____.

Joanna has

_____.

b 🎧 1/55 Listen again and complete the chart.

	Kelly	Joanna
1 birthday		
2 appearance		
3 favorite movie		
4 favorite actor		
5 favorite singer		

Speak

5 PAIRS Compare your physical features with those of your parents. Answer these questions:

What are the similarities between you and your parents? What are the differences?

My father has straight hair, but my mother has curly hair. I have curly hair just like my mother!

Write

6 Read the factfile. Then, on a piece of paper, write about the Sprouse twins. Use the article about the Phelps twins as a model.

Names: Dylan and Cole Sprouse
Jobs: Actors
TV show: *The Suite Life of Zack and Cody*
Identical twins? Yes
Favorite sport: Basketball
Dylan's favorite movie: *Godzilla*
Cole's favorite movie: *Little Shop of Horrors*
Good friends: Yes

CLIL PROJECT, page 140

Grammar (40 points)

1 Fill in the blanks with the correct form of *there is* or *there are*. (14 points)

Teacher: This is the student hotel. ⁰ ___There are___ six beds in each room.

Laura: How many bathrooms ¹ _____?

Teacher: ² _____ three bathrooms.

David: ³ _____ any showers?

Teacher: Yes, ⁴ _____ . ⁵ _____ some showers over there.

Laura: ⁶ _____ a washing machine?

Teacher: No, ⁷ _____ . And ⁸ _____ a dishwasher. Sorry.

David: ⁹ _____ a TV room?

Teacher: Yes, ¹⁰ _____ . And ¹¹ _____ a CD player, too.

David: Great. ¹² _____ any CDs?

Teacher: No, ¹³ _____ . Unfortunately ¹⁴ _____ any CDs or DVDs.

2 Look at the pictures. Write sentences telling where the phone is. (5 points)

0 ___It's in front of___ the computer.

1 _____ the sofa.

2 _____ the chair.

3 _____ the bag.

4 _____ the wastebasket.

5 _____ the mirror.

3 Circle the correct answer: a), b), or c). (5 points)

0 Their house is very nice but there isn't _____ garage.
   (a) a   b) an   c) the

1 It's _____ old house but it's very pretty.
   a) a   b) an   c) the

2 There are _____ nice photos of you here.
   a) some   b) a   c) any

3 Wow! _____ yard is very big!
   a) A   b) Any   c) The

4 There aren't _____ new students in our class.
   a) some   b) a   c) any

5 Are there _____ good DVDs?
   a) the   b) any   c) an

4 Write sentences with the correct form of *have* and *a*, *some*, or *any*. (5 points)
(✓) = affirmative (✗) = negative (?) = question

0 I/new CDs. (✓) ___I have some new CDs.___

1 She/brothers or sisters. (✗) _____

2 Joe/cell phone (?) _____

3 You/great bedroom! (✓) _____

4 They/good DVDs. (✗) _____

5 We/chocolate (?) _____

5 Answer the questions using the short form. (5 points)

0 Does Anna have red hair? (✓) ___Yes, she does.___

1 Do you have 50 cents? (✗) _____

2 Do we have Math today? (✓) _____

3 Do they have your phone number? (✗) _____

4 Does he have eyeglasses? (✓) _____

5 Do I have your e-mail address? (✗) _____

6 Complete the paragraph. (6 points)

⁰ ___There's___ a big poster of Shakira ¹ _____ my bedroom wall. Shakira is a singer from Colombia. She ² _____ long, blond, wavy hair and brown eyes. She and I ³ _____ the same sign. Her birthday is ⁴ _____ February 2, and my birthday is ⁵ _____ February, too. She ⁶ _____ any brothers or sisters—she's an only child.

Vocabulary (40 points)

7 Write the words from the box in the correct rows. (24 points)

> • armchair • ~~bathroom~~ • bedroom • blond
> • brown • cabinet • daughter • desk • door
> • fair • fall • floor • gray • husband • kitchen
> • sofa • son • spring • summer • table • wall
> • wife • window • winter • yard

Parts of the house/rooms	*bathroom*
Furniture	
Hair color	
Family	
Seasons	

8 Solve the clues to the crossword puzzle and find the hidden word (number 8). (8 points)

⁰E Y E G L A ⁸S S E S
¹B E   F
²C
³B
⁴M   -
⁵L
⁶S
⁷M

Clues

0 He has *eyeglasses*.
1 She is _____.
2 He has _____ hair.
3 He has a _____.
4 She has _____ hair.
5 She has _____ hair.
6 He has _____ hair.
7 He has a _____.
8 Hidden word: _____

9 Write the full dates. (8 points)

0 – 8/6   *August sixth/August 6*
1 – 2/13 _____
2 – 9/1 _____
3 – 7/3 _____
4 – 4/2 _____

Use your English (20 points)

10 Complete each conversation with a phrase from the box. (10 points)

> • What's playing? • Let's see.
> • In your dreams! • not really my kind of music.
> • ~~I'm not sure.~~ • sorry.

0 **A:** Is Selena Gomez in that movie?
  B: *I'm not sure.*
1 **A:** Oh, look! A Coldplay CD! **B:** Oh, that's
  _____
2 **A:** He's very good-looking, like me.
  B: _____
3 **A:** I have some good photos here. **B:** _____
4 **A:** Here's the theater. **B:** _____
5 **A:** Are there any CDs? **B:** No, _____

11 Look at the jumbled conversations below. Number the lines in the correct order. (10 points)

Conversation 1

_____ a) How old are they?
_____ b) I have two brothers.
_____ c) Neil is 16 and Benny is 12.
_____ d) Neil and Benny.
_____ e) What are their names?
_*1*_ f) How many brothers do you have?

Conversation 2

_____ a) Sure. Here you go.
_____ b) Great. Can I borrow it?
_*1*_ c) Do you have a CD player?
_____ d) No, I'm sorry. I need it.
_____ e) Yes, I do.
_____ f) Thanks. And can I borrow your laptop, too?

I don't work here.

Grammar Simple present with *I, you, we, they*
Vocabulary Occupations
Function Ask and answer questions about your personal information

Get started

1 What occupations do you know?

Vocabulary: Occupations

2 (2 02) Listen and repeat. Label the pictures.

- artist • chef • doctor • plumber • secretary
- waiter/waitress

1

secretary

2

_____

3

_____

4

_____

5

_____

6

_____

3 (2 03) Listen and repeat. Write the equivalent word in your language for each word below.

1 dentist _____
2 actor _____
3 nurse _____
4 singer _____
5 police officer _____
6 salesclerk _____
7 teacher _____
8 builder/carpenter _____

Presentation

4 (2 04) Listen and read along. Circle the occupations.

Zach: OK, guys, here are your snacks.
Laura: Thanks. Hey, Zach, **do** you **work** here at the youth club during the day, too?
Zach: No, I **don't**. I **work** in a hospital. I'm a nurse.
David: So, you're a nurse, a youth coordinator, and a waiter?
Zach: Very funny!
Polly: Where **do** you **live**?
Zach: In Seattle, but my parents **live** in Cuba.
Polly: Cuba? Cool!
Zach: Yeah, but they **don't live** there all the time. They **live** here with me in the summer.
Polly: **Do** you **speak** Spanish?
Zach: Yes, I **do**, and a little Portuguese.
Carlos: Hey, Zach! The faucet's broken!
Zach: Don't look at me! I'm not a plumber!

Grammar

Simple present with *I, you, we, they*	
Affirmative	**Negative**
I **work** there.	I **don't work** here.
Questions	**Short answers**
Do you **work** there?	Yes, I **do**./No, I **don't**.
Where do they work?	In the hospital.

☞ Go to page 132, Master your grammar.

Practice

7 Complete the conversations.

1 (live)
   A: Where ____*do*____ you ____*live*____?
   B: I ____*live*____ in New York.

2 (speak)
   A: _____ you _____ English?
   B: Yes, I _____ . I _____ English and
   Spanish.

3 (work)
   A: Where _____ your parents _____?
   B: They _____ in the city.

4 (live)
   A: _____ you _____ in a house?
   B: No, I _____ . I _____ in an apartment.

5 (study)
   A: What languages _____ you _____ at
   school?
   B: We _____ English and Spanish.

Speak

8 **PAIRS** Ask your partner the questions from
Exercise 7.

Write

9 Write about yourself on a piece of paper. Use
the questions in Exercise 7 for ideas. Add other
information.

Phrases

2 05 Listen and repeat.

- Cool! • Very funny! • Don't look at me!
- OK, guys.

Comprehension

5 Complete the word web about Zach.

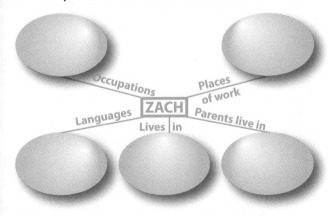

Solve it!

6 Look at the photo. Zach has one more
occupation. What is it?

Extra practice
- **Student Book, page 116, Lesson 5A**
- **Language Builder: WB page 34; GB, page 112**
- **Student CD-ROM, Unit 5**

Grammar	Simple present with *he, she, it*
Vocabulary	Places of work
Function	Ask and answer questions about someone

Get started

1 Look at the photo below. What can you see? Do you think the hole in the street is dangerous?

Read

2 (2/06) Listen and read along. What kind of artist is Julian Beever?

Street art lives!

Julian Beever **is** from the U.K., but he **lives** in Belgium now. Where does he work? He **doesn't work** in an office or a studio; he **works** outside on the street. What does he do? He's a sidewalk artist. He **makes** 3D (three-dimensional) drawings on sidewalks in cities all over the world.

Julian **makes** his drawings with chalk. He **works** eight hours a day. How long does a drawing take? One drawing **takes** about three days. When it **rains**, the drawing **disappears**. Luckily, he **takes** a photo of every drawing.

Comprehension

3 Cover the reading. Read these statements. Which information comes first? Number 1–7.

_____ 1 Julian makes his drawings with chalk.

_____ 2 He lives in Belgium now.

_____ 3 He's a sidewalk artist.

_____ 4 One drawing takes three days to do.

_1_ 5 Julian Beever is from the U.K.

_____ 6 Luckily, he takes a photo of every drawing.

_____ 7 When it rains, the drawing disappears.

Grammar

Simple present with *he, she, it*	
Affirmative	**Negative**
He **works** outside.	He **doesn't work** outside.
Questions	**Short answers**
Does he **work** outside?	Yes, he **does**. No, he **doesn't**.
Where **does** he **work**?	On the street.

☞ Go to page 132, Master your grammar.

Pronunciation: /ʌ/ d<u>oe</u>s

4 🎧 Go to page 126.

Practice

5 In your notebook, write questions about Julian Beever.

1 Where/he live now?

2 he/work in an office?

3 Where/he work?

4 What/he do?

5 What/he use to draw?

6 How long/drawing take?

7 he/take a photo of his drawings?

Speak

6 PAIRS Ask your partner the questions in Exercise 5.

A: *Where does he live now?*

B: *He lives in Belgium.*

7 PAIRS Complete the text. Then ask your partner three questions about Jaycee.

> • not/want • not/be
> • live • work • go • be (x2)

An American in London

Jaycee [1] _is_ a student. She [2] _____ in an apartment in London.
She [3] _____ from the U.K.
She [4] _____ from California, in the U.S. Her dad [5] _____ in an American bank. She [6] _____ home to California for vacation, but she [7] _____ to live there. Life in the U.K. is great!

Vocabulary: Places of work

8 Listen and repeat.

> • construction site • hospital • kitchen • office
> • restaurant • school • store/mall • studio

9 PAIRS Take turns asking where these people work.

1 doctor 2 secretary 3 teacher 4 waiter/waitress

5 artist 6 salesclerk 7 chef 8 builder

A: *Where does a doctor work?*

B: *A doctor works in a hospital.*

💡 Solve it!

10 Listen and guess the occupation.

Write

11 On a piece of paper, write about the jobs of three family members.

My mother's a teacher. She works in a school . . .

> ▶ **Extra practice**
> • **Student Book, page 117, Lesson 5B**
> • **Language Builder: WB page 36; GB, page 113**
> • **Student CD-ROM, Unit 5**

5c I love him.

Grammar	Object pronouns: *me, you, him, her, it, us, them*
Vocabulary	Adjectives of opinion
Function	Exchange opinions

Get started

1 Who are your favorite actors and singers?

 Solve it!

2 Guess who the celebrities in the photos are.

I think Number 1 is Zac Efron.

Guess who they are!

Presentation

3 [🎧 2/11] Listen and read along. How many celebrities do they talk about?

Polly: David, look at this.

David: It's a quiz. You have to guess who the celebrities are. I think Number 1 is Zac Efron. What do you think of **him**?

Polly: I love him. I think he's really good. And he's so cute! What about you?

David: I don't like **him**. I think he's boring. I like Demi Lovato.

Polly: Oh, yeah, Number 2 is Demi. She's great. I think Number 3 is the Jonas Brothers. I like **them**. What do you think of **them**?

David: I'm not sure. Oh. That's Lady Gaga!

Polly: I don't like **her** at all. I think she's awful.

David: Me, too!

Comprehension

4 Who do Polly and David like? Put a check (✓), an ✗, or a question mark (?) in the correct box.

	Polly	David
Zac Efron	✓	
Demi Lovato		
the Jonas Brothers		
Lady Gaga		

Grammar

Subject pronouns	Object pronouns
I	me
you	you
he	him
she	her
it	it
we	us
they	them

☛ Go to page 132, Master your grammar.

Practice

5 Replace the underlined words with the correct object pronoun.

them
1 David loves <u>hamburgers</u>.

2 Laura doesn't like <u>soda</u>.

3 I'm not sure about <u>Taylor Swift</u>.

4 She really likes <u>me and my sister</u>.

5 What does Laura think of <u>Zach</u>?

6a Write about David and Laura's likes and dislikes. Use *but* in your sentences.

✓✓ = love ✓ = like ✗ = not like
✗✗ = hate ? = not sure about

	David	Laura	You
1 rap music	✓	?	
2 video games	✓✓	✗	
3 Zac Efron	✗	?	
4 Lady Gaga	✗	✓	

1 Rap music: *David likes it, but Laura isn't sure about it.*

2 Video games: _____

3 Zac Efron: _____

4 Lady Gaga: _____

b **PAIRS** What about your likes and dislikes? Fill in the *You* column. Then compare with a partner.

Vocabulary: Adjectives of opinion

7  Listen and repeat. Then put the adjectives under the correct face.

• awesome • awful • bad • boring • cool • funny • good • great • incredible • terrible • weird

😃	😠
_good_____	_____
_____	_____

Use your English: Exchange opinions

8  Listen and repeat. Then practice the conversation.

A: What do you think of Taylor Swift, Danny?

B: I don't like her. I think she's boring.

C: Me, too. What about you, Maya?

A: I love her! I think she's great.

Taylor Swift

Ask for an opinion
• What do you think of . . . ? / What about you?

Give a positive opinion
• I love . . . / I like . . .
• I think she's good/cool/awesome.
• I think she's a/an good/great/incredible singer.

Give a negative opinion
• I hate . . . / I don't like . . .
• I think he/she's boring/awful.
• I think he/she's a bad/terrible singer.

9 **PAIRS** Ask questions about two of your favorite celebrities.

Write

10 On a piece of paper, write your opinion about a famous celebrity.

 Extra practice
• Student Book, page 117, Lesson 5C
• Language Builder: WB, page 38; GB, page 114
• Student CD-ROM, Unit 5

INTEGRATED
CONSOLIDATION
SKILLS

Values for living

Get started

1 Read the work information about American teenagers.

2 GROUPS Talk about these questions:

1 What is your opinion of 13- and 14-year-olds working?

2 What job would you like to have as an 11- to 13-year-old?

In the U.S., if you are 13 or younger, you can deliver newspapers, baby-sit, or work as an actor.

If you are 14 and older, you can work in movie theaters, stores, or restaurants.

Read

3 Read about Sally, Edward, and Madeline. Who can't have a job at the Mega Pizza restaurant?

WHAT IS THE RIGHT THING TO DO?

Sally is 16 years old. She gets a Saturday job at the Mega Pizza restaurant. She likes the job, and she works hard. The customers like her. One day, Sally breaks some glasses by accident. The manager, Mr. Hammond, doesn't see the accident.

Edward is also 16 years old. He gets a Saturday job at the Mega Pizza restaurant. Edward has five brothers and sisters, and his family is poor. At the end of his shift one evening, there are three uneaten pizzas on the kitchen table. Edward wants to take the pizzas home for his family.

Madeline is 13 years and nine months old, and she's in eighth grade. She wants a job at the Mega Pizza restaurant. She talks to Mr. Hammond. He asks her age.

New words
- deliver • newspaper • baby-sit
- get/want a job • work hard
- customer • manager • break
- glass • by accident • poor
- uneaten • shift • talk • ask

Comprehension

4 Give short answers.

1 Does Sally like her job? _____

2 What does Sally do by accident? _____

3 Is Edward's family rich? _____

4 What does Edward want to do with the uneaten pizzas? _____

5 How old is Madeline? _____

6 Is she a student? _____

Speak your mind!

> **Speaking tip: Speak clearly**
>
> When you speak, speak clearly and look at the person you are talking to. This makes it easier for the person to understand you.

5 **GROUPS** Discuss the situations below. What is the right thing to do, and what is the wrong thing to do?

I think Number 1 is the wrong thing to do.

1 Sally puts the broken glasses in the trash and doesn't tell Mr. Hammond.

2 Sally tells Mr. Hammond and apologizes.

3 Edward takes the pizzas home to his family. He doesn't ask Mr. Hammond.

4 Edward takes the pizzas home to his family. He asks Mr. Hammond first.

5 Madeline tells Mr. Hammond her real age.

6 Madeline tells Mr. Hammond she's 14.

> **Learning strategy: Predict from the task**
>
> Look at the task before you listen. Try to predict some of the words you might hear. This will help you understand more the first time you listen.

Listen

6 🎧 2/14 Listen and correct the mistakes.

1 Mr. Hammond asks Sally for ~~eight~~ *six* glasses.

Sally breaks the glasses. She tells Mr. Hammond.

2 Edward doesn't work hard. He sees three pizzas on the kitchen table. He takes them home to his family. He doesn't ask Mr. Hammond.

3 Madeline interviews with Mr. Hammond. She says that she is 15. Mr. Hammond doesn't give her a job.

7 🎧 2/14 Listen again and answer the questions.

1 What question does Mr. Hammond ask Sally?

_____

2 What question does Edward ask Mr. Hammond?

_____

3 Write one question Mr. Hammond asks Madeline.

_____

Write

8a Complete the blog post with the words below.

> • deliver • pick up • read • see • thirteen

> Hi. I'm _____. On weekends, I
> _____ newspapers in my neighborhood.
> Every morning, I _____ a man
> _____ his neighbor's newspaper and
> _____ it. What's the right thing for me to do?
> Posted by José Luis on August 9, 2011 @7 P.M.

b Write a comment on what José Luis can do.

> José Luis, I think you can _____
> _____
> Comment by _____ on August 9, 2011 @8 P.M.

CLIL PROJECT, page 140

Grammar	Simple present with fixed times
	Preposition of time: *at*
Vocabulary	Clock times
Function	Talk about the times of events

Get started

1 GROUPS Discuss these questions:

Are you the type of person who's always on time, or one who's always late?

Why do you like to always be on time?

Why are you always late?

Presentation

2 🎧 2/15 Listen and read along.

David: What time **does** the tour **start**?

Carlos: **At** eleven thirty—more or less.

Polly: And what time is it now?

Laura: Eleven twenty-five.

Polly: Oh, no! We're late and the tour is only thirty minutes! Let's hurry!

In Safeco Field

Guide: Hello. Welcome to Seattle's Safeco Field—home of the Seattle Mariners.

David: Wow! Uh, . . . when's the next game?

Guide: It's on Saturday. It **starts** at three o'clock. Ichiro Suzuki is playing.

Carlos: Really? He's the best! He's a recipient of the Gold Glove and the Silver Slugger Awards. He's also an All Star in the Major League Baseball All-Star Game.

Polly: Amazing!

David: Oh, man! I really have to see that game.

Phrases

🎧 1/16 Listen and repeat.

- Oh man! • Welcome . . .
- Let's hurry! • Amazing!

Comprehension

3 Circle the correct answer.

1 The friends are **at a baseball game** / **on a tour** of the baseball field.

2 Safeco Field is the home field of the **Seattle Mariners** / **the Boston Red Sox**.

3 Ichiro Suzuki is **a baseball player** / **the tour guide**.

4 Ichiro Suzuki won the Gold Glove Award in **2007** / **2009**.

Vocabulary: Clock times

4 Listen and repeat.

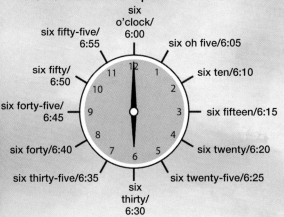

six o'clock/ 6:00
six fifty-five/ 6:55
six oh five/6:05
six fifty/ 6:50
six ten/6:10
six forty-five/ 6:45
six fifteen/6:15
six forty/6:40
six twenty/6:20
six thirty-five/6:35
six twenty-five/6:25
six thirty/ 6:30

5 PAIRS Take turns. Ask for the time.

1 6:45

A: *What time is it?*
B: *It's six forty-five.*

2 10:15	4 4:00	6 1:50	8 12:10
3 3:30	5 8:20	7 11:25	9 7:55

Solve it!

6 Read the conversation again. What time does the tour end?

Grammar

Simple present with fixed times
Preposition of time: *at*

Questions	Answers
What time **does** it **start**?	It **starts at** 11:30 A.M.
What time **does** it **end**?	It **ends at** 5 P.M.

Verbs usually followed by fixed times

• start • end • open • close • leave • arrive

Note
A.M. = morning; P.M. = afternoon/night

☞ Go to page 133, Master your grammar.

Practice

7 You win a weekend in London. Look at the information. In your notebook, write questions about the times. Use these cues:

1 The plane to London (*leave/arrive*)

A: *What time does the plane to London leave?*
B: *It leaves at seven o'clock in the morning.*

2 Breakfast at the hotel (*start/end*)
3 The British Museum (*open/close*)
4 The plane to Seattle (*leave/arrive*)

A

Fly Away Travel

July 12			
From	**Depart**	**To**	**Arrive**
Seattle	7:00 A.M.	London	5:00 P.M.
July 14			
From	**Depart**	**To**	**Arrive**
London	4:45 A.M.	Seattle	3:15 P.M.

B
Breakfast
is from 7:30 – 9:45

C
THE BRITISH
MUSEUM
9:00 - 5:00

Speak

8 PAIRS Think of three Saturday TV shows. Ask your partner what time each show starts and ends.

Write

9 In your notebook, write about your favorite TV shows. Use the information from Exercise 8.

Extra practice
• Student Book, page 117, Lesson 6A
• Language Builder: WB, page 42; GB, page 116
• Student CD-ROM, Unit 6

6B I'm never late.

Grammar Adverbs of frequency
Vocabulary Daily routines
Function Talk about daily routines

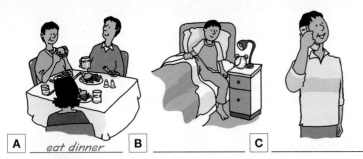

A _eat dinner_ B _____ C _____

D _____ E _____ F _____

G _____ H _____ I _____

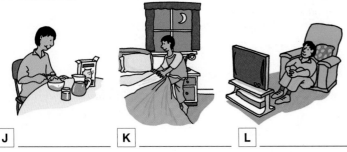

J _____ K _____ L _____

M _____ N _____ O _____

50

Get started

1 What time do you get up? What time do you go to bed?

Vocabulary: Daily routines

2 🎧 (2/18) Listen and repeat. Then label the pictures on the left with phrases from the box.

- brush my teeth • call a friend • do my homework
- eat breakfast • eat dinner • eat lunch
- get home • get up • go home • go to bed
- go to school • listen to music • read in bed
- take a shower • watch TV

💡 Solve it!

3 What do pictures B, D, F, J, and N have in common?

Read

4 🎧 (2/19) Listen and read about a Russian teenager's daily routine. Fill in the blanks with the clock times. Then listen and check your answers.

- 9:30 P.M. • 1 P.M. • 8:30 A.M. • 10:30 P.M.
- 6:30 P.M. • 8 o'clock • 7:00 P.M.

SHARING
CULTURES

What's it like to be a teenager in modern Russia? Fourteen-year-old Anton Morozov from Moscow tells us about his daily routine.

My morning is the same every day. I **always** get up at [1] _8 o'clock_. Then I take a shower and brush my teeth. I eat breakfast with my parents at about [2] _____. We **usually have** cereal, eggs, and bread. But **sometimes** we **have** pancakes with honey and sour cream — it's my favorite breakfast! Then my grandmother arrives to stay with me, and my parents go to work.

In Moscow students go to school either in the morning or the afternoon. I don't go to school in

Comprehension

5 Complete Anton's daily routines.

Morning	Afternoon	Evening
1 *get up*	1 *eat lunch*	1 *get home*
2	2	2
3	3	3
4	4	4
5 *do homework*	5 *get to school*	5 *read in bed*

Grammar

Adverbs of frequency

always   usually   often   sometimes   hardly ever   never

Position of adverbs

<u>Before</u> the main verb: I **always** <u>get up</u> at eight o'clock.
<u>After</u> the verb *to be*: <u>I'm</u> **usually** very hungry.

☞ Go to page 133, Master your grammar.

the morning. I **usually do** my homework after breakfast. I go to school after lunch. On the way to school I **often call** my friends on my cell phone and listen to music. School starts at ³ _____ . **I'm never** late. School ends at ⁴ _____ .

When I get home at ⁵ _____ , **I'm usually** very hungry so I eat dinner. After dinner I watch TV. I go to bed at ⁶ _____ and read in bed. **I'm hardly ever** asleep before ⁷ _____ .

Practice

6 **PAIRS** Take turns asking and answering about Anton's day.

1 What time/get up?
   A: *What time does he get up?*
   B: *He always gets up at eight..*
2 What/have for breakfast?
3 What/do in the morning?
4 What/do on his way to school?
5 What/do/get home?
6 What/do after dinner?

Listen

7 🎧 Listen to Carlos and Polly. Complete the chart.

Bedtime	Carlos	Polly
Goes to bed at . . .		
Before going to sleep . . .		
Goes to sleep at . . .		

Speak

8a **PAIRS** Ask your partner about his or her daily routine. Use the questions in Exercise 6. Take notes.

b **GROUPS** Tell another pair about your partner's routine.

Write

9a On a piece of paper, list your morning and afternoon routines on Saturdays.

b Using the information in Exercise 9a, write a paragraph about your Saturday routine.

> **Extra practice**
> • Student Book, page 117, Lesson 6B
> • Language Builder: WB, page 44; GB, page 117
> • Student CD-ROM, Unit 6

6c

How often do you . . . ?

Grammar	Adverbial expressions of frequency
Function	Express surprise and comment

Get started

1 **PAIRS** Discuss: Are watching TV and playing video games bad habits? Why or why not?

Read

2a Do the Good and Bad Habits Quiz. Put a check (✓) in the appropriate column.

b **PAIRS** Now ask your partner the questions in the quiz. Use a different color pen and note his or her answers.

A: *How often do you get up early?*

B: *I get up early every day.*

The Good and Bad Habits Quiz

How often do you . . .	A Every day		B Twice or three times a week		C Once a month		D Never	
	Me	You	Me	You	Me	You	Me	You
1 get up early?								
2 eat fast food?								
3 hang out with your family?								
4 watch TV?								
5 eat some fruit?								
6 go to bed very late?								
7 read a book or a magazine in English?								
8 play video games?								
9 play a sport or exercise?								
10 text someone during class?								

Check your score

Questions 1, 3, 5, 7, 9:
Score 3 points for *A*, 2 points for *B*, 1 point for *C*, and 0 points for *D*.

Questions 2, 4, 6, 8, 10:
Score 0 points for *A*, 1 point for *B*, 2 points for *C*, and 3 points for *D*.

What does your score mean?

20–30 points: You have a lot of good habits, but don't forget to enjoy yourself once or twice a week.

10–19 points: OK, you aren't perfect. You have some good habits and some bad habits, but you're pretty good.

0–9 points: Oh, dear! Is it time to change?

Grammar

Adverbial expressions of frequency

How often do you watch TV?

I watch TV every day/twice a week.

every		day
once		week
twice	a	month
three times		year

☛ Go to page 133, Master your grammar.

Practice

3 Write sentences using the cues.

1 | tennis | I | week | play | twice | a

I play tennis twice a week.

2 | gets | early | Carlos | day | up | every

_____

3 | times | month | They | a | exercise | three

_____

4 | week | to | John | late | a | goes | bed | once

_____

4a **GROUPS** Join another pair. Tell the group about your and your partner's habits, using the answers to quiz items 1–5 on page 52.

I get up early every day on school days, and Mario gets up early, too.

b Student B, do the same thing but using the answers to quiz items 6–10.

I never go to bed very late, but Juan Carlos goes to bed late every day.

Listen

5a Listen to Simon and Hannah. How many good habits does Simon have?

b Listen again and complete the chart.

How often does	Simon	Hannah
1 eat fast food?		
2 eat fruit?		
3 exercise?		

Pronunciation: /o/ open

6 Go to page 126.

Use your English: Express surprise and comment

7 **PAIRS** Listen and repeat. Then practice the conversation.

A: How often do you exercise?
B: Every day.
A: Every day? Wow! That's great.
B: What about you? How often do you exercise?
A: About once a month.
B: Really? That's not good.

Express surprise	Comment positively
• Really?	• That's great!
• Seriously?	• That's good.
• Wow!	• That's interesting.
• You're kidding!	• That's awesome!
• Every day?	**Comment negatively**
	• That's not good.
	• That's awful.

8 Ask questions with *How often . . . ?* and the phrases below. Express surprise and comment.

• get up very late • help around the house
• clean your bedroom • go to bed early

Write

9 On a piece of paper, write about three good habits and two bad habits you have. Use the information on page 52.

I have some good and some bad habits. Some of my good habits are . . .

 Extra practice
• **Student Book, page 117, Lesson 6C**
• **Language Builder: WB, page 46; GB, page 117**
• **Student CD-ROM, Unit 6**

School life in the U.S.

Get started

1 What's your day like on school days? Do you have time for breakfast?

Read

2 Read the text. How many classes does Emily have in a school day?

An American student's life

Emily is in middle school in the U.S. She's 13. This is her typical day.

On school days, Emily gets up at 6 A.M. She doesn't have time for breakfast. She drinks milk and is out of the house by 7:00. She waits for the school bus near her house. It arrives at 7:15. Her first class starts at 8:00. She has four classes in the morning.

Lunch is from noon to 1:00 P.M. Emily and her friends have lunch in the cafeteria. Afternoon classes start at one. Emily has two afternoon classes.

School ends at 3:00 P.M., but Emily doesn't get home until 7 o'clock. She has a lot of activities, such as school clubs and sports. When does Emily do her homework? She starts at 8:00 and finishes at 11:00. She usually goes on her Facebook page to check messages from her classmates about homework. She and her friends also text each other about homework.

On Fridays, Emily volunteers at an animal shelter. She has a favorite dog there. She takes him out for walks and plays with him. On Saturdays, Emily is also very busy. She has violin lessons, karate, and soccer practice. Sundays are "free days" for Emily. It's a day for shopping, going to the movies, or just hanging out.

New words
- middle school • typical • corner • messages • volunteer
- animal shelter • violin • karate • hang out • middle school
- high school • required • subjects • uniform • electives

U.S. Secondary Education Factfile

Most students in the U.S., rich or poor, go to public schools.

Middle School

6th Grade	ages 11–12
7th Grade	ages 12–13
8th Grade	ages 13–14

High School

9th Grade (Freshman)	ages 14–15
10th Grade (Sophomore)	ages 15–16
11th Grade (Junior)	ages 16–17
12th Grade (Senior)	ages 17–18

Uniform

Public school students don't wear uniforms.

Required subjects

Science	Math
English and literature	Social science
Foreign languages	Physical education

Electives *(Students can choose)*

Visual arts (painting, photography, etc.)

Performing arts (drama, band, dance, etc.)

Computer science

Comprehension

3 Complete the chart about Emily's school day.

Morning	Afternoon/Evening
Gets up at _____	Lunch starts at _____
↓	↓
Leaves the house at _____	Class starts at _____
↓	↓
The school bus arrives at _____	School ends at _____
↓	↓
Class starts at _____	Gets home at _____

4 Copy the chart in your notebook. Fill in the boxes with your own information.

5 Complete Column 1 below with Emily's activities. Complete Column 2 with yours.

	Emily	You
Fridays	volunteers at animal shelter	
Saturdays		
Sundays		

Listen

6a 🔊 2/25 Listen and complete the chart.

Emily . . .	Kevin . . .
1 leaves home at 7:00.	
2 eats in the cafeteria.	
3 has lunch with friends.	
4 school ends at 3:00.	
5 gets home at 7:00.	

b What part of Emily's and Kevin's school day is the same? _____

_____

Learning strategy: Ask questions to learn about a new culture

When you are in another country, don't be afraid to ask locals specific questions about their country or culture. You can then learn about the new culture and practice your English as well.

Speak

7a Complete the questions in your notebook.

1 What time/start/school?
   A: *What time do you start school?*
2 How many classes/be there/in one day?
3 What time/have/lunch? Where/have it?
4 Be/there any school clubs or sports clubs?
5 What/be/your favorite subjects?

b PAIRS Take turns asking and answering the questions in Exercise 7a.

Write

Writing tip: *and, but, because, so*

Use ***and*, *but*, *because*,** and ***so*** to combine two parts of a sentence.

Emily leaves home at seven **and** waits for the bus.

School ends at 3:00, **but** Emily gets home at 7:00.

Emily volunteers at an animal shelter **because** she loves animals.

She is free on Sundays, **so** she goes to the movies.

8 In your notebook combine these sentences with *and, but, because,* or *so*.

1 Emily gets up at six o'clock. She takes a shower.
2 She's usually late. She always runs to the bus stop.
3 She gets up late. She goes to bed late!
4 Emily takes her cell phone to school. She keeps it in her locker.
5 I play sports after school. I don't get home before five.

9 Write about your school day on a piece of paper. Use *and, but, so,* and *because* whenever appropriate. Use Emily's information for ideas.

CLIL PROJECT, page 140

Review: Units 5 & 6

Grammar (40 points)

1 Complete the sentences with the correct form of a verb from the box. (8 points)

> • not live • ~~speak~~ • not speak • be • go
> • ~~not be~~ • work • not work • want • not go

0 My father and mother _____*speak*_____ English.

00 I *'m not* _____ from Madrid, but I live there.

1 He's a teacher. He _____ in a school in Quito.

2 We _____ in Brazil. We live in the U.S.

3 Our teacher _____ from Korea.

4 I _____ Italian. I only speak English.

5 My parents _____ to live in Belize. They love it.

6 My best friend _____ to school in Seattle.

7 My mother _____ on Friday. It's her day off.

8 In the U.S., children _____ to school on Saturday.

2 Replace the underlined words with the words in parentheses. Then rewrite the sentences in your notebook. (6 points)

0 *The students* are from Italy. (Maria)
  Maria is from Italy.

1 Where do *your parents* live? (Paul)

2 *John* doesn't study Russian. (We)

3 Do *they* speak Spanish? (Lucy)

4 What music do *they* like? (Jack)

5 Is *he* from Toronto? (They)

6 *The girls* go to school in London. (Anna)

3 Complete the sentences with *me, her, him, it, us,* or *them.* (6 points)

0 I like this school but Carol doesn't like ___*it*___ .

1 Helena doesn't like Justin, but I like _____ !

2 Those are mine. Can I have _____ , please?

3 I like Carla and she likes _____ ! We're friends.

4 I think Beyoncé's great! Do you like _____ ?

5 My grandmother lives in our house with _____ .

6 My sister likes coffee but I don't like _____ .

4 Use the times in the chart to make questions. (8 points)

	Leave	Arrive	Open	Close	Start	End
bus	6:30	7:00				
train	11:30	12:45				
store			9:00	6:00		
bank			9:30	4:00		
game					3:00	4:30
concert					7:15	10:00

0 At six-thirty
  What time does the bus leave?

1 At seven o'clock _____

2 At eleven-thirty _____

3 At three o'clock _____

4 At seven-fifteen _____

5 At nine o'clock _____

6 At four o'clock _____

7 At six o'clock _____

8 At four-thirty _____

5 Rewrite the sentences in your notebook. Put the adverbs of frequency in the correct position. (5 points)

0 They have coffee after lunch. (always)
  They always have coffee after lunch.

1 I go to my bank on Tuesdays. (usually)

2 She gets up before eight o'clock. (never)

3 I'm late for school. (often)

4 She goes swimming after school. (sometimes)

5 He plays video games. (hardly ever)

6 Complete the e-mail with the missing words. (7 points)

000

Hi Sandra!

My name is Eva and I ⁰ *live* in Chicago. My parents ¹_____ at the city hospital. My brother Michael is 18. He ²_____ go to high school. He ³_____ to college. What ⁴_____ you usually do after school? I do my homework, and then I ⁵_____ video games! ⁶_____ you like country music? I love Carrie Underwood. Do you like ⁷_____?

I hope to hear from you soon.

Best wishes,

Eva

Vocabulary (40 points)

7 Fill in the missing vowels to make occupations. Then draw lines to match the occupations to their places of work. (14 points)

0 art_i_st   a) school
1 n_rs_   b) construction site
2 b_ _ld_r   c) office
3 w_ _t_r   d) store
4 s_l_s cl_rk   e) hospital
5 t_ _ ch_r   f) restaurant
6 s_cr_t_ry   g) studio
7 ch_f   h) kitchen

8 Unscramble the words to make jobs. (6 points)

0 HECF _____CHEF_____

1 RACTO _____

2 STRIAT _____

3 TSIDNE _____

4 GSNEIR _____

5 CRODOT _____

6 MULPREB _____

9 Find and circle ten more adjectives in the wordsearch. (10 points)

```
N  H  X  A  W  E  S  O  M  E
I  N  C  R  E  D  I  B  L  E
M  B  O  R  I  N  G  H  T  L
Y  R  R  F  P  H  F  C  E  L
A  W  F  U  L  X  C  P  R  F
K  G  W  N  M  W  E  I  R  D
C  R  B  N  Q  P  L  B  I  B
O  E  A  Y  G  O  O  D  B  T
O  A  D  D  Q  R  R  W  L  R
L  T  T  F  R  N  M  Y  E  M
```

10 Draw a line to match the verb with the correct phrase to make daily routines. (10 points)

0 get   a) the radio; music
1 play   b) breakfast; lunch; dinner
2 go to   c) TV; a DVD
3 watch   d) school; bed
4 listen to   e) up; home; to school
5 eat   f) video games; soccer

Use your English (20 points)

11 Circle the correct response. (10 points)

0 **A:** Look. I have Shakira's phone number!
  B: a) Let's hurry! b) Very funny!
      c) Don't look at me!

1 **A:** My cousin's a movie star.
  B: a) Great job! b) You're kidding!
      c) What do you think?

2 **A:** The movie was really good!
  B: a) Hurry up! b) Oh, man. I have to see it!
      c) Get up!

3 **A:** Where's my cell phone?
  B: a) Amazing! b) Wow! c) Don't look at me!

4 **A:** Look! I got an A on my math test!
  B: a) That's awful! b) That's great!
      c) Welcome to our house!

5 **A:** The bus is leaving in five minutes!
  B: a) Let's hurry! b) That's good.
      c) What about you?

12 Look at the scrambled conversation below. Number the lines in the correct order. (10 points)

_____ a) *El Cantante*? Who's in it?

_____ b) Me, too. What do you think of Marc Anthony?

_____ c) J-Lo? She's OK, but I don't like her music. What about you?

_____ d) It's called *El Cantante*.

_____ e) Jennifer Lopez and Marc Anthony. What do you think of J-Lo?

_____ f) I think he's cool. What do *you* think of him?

_____ g) I don't like her music either, but I like her movies.

_____ h) I think he's boring.

_____ i) Yeah, sure. What movie is it?

__1__ j) Hi. Do you want to watch my new DVD?

_____ k) You're kidding! He's great.

SELF-CHECK	
Grammar	_____ /40
Vocabulary	_____ /40
Use your English	_____ /20
Total score	_____ /100

Can you run five miles?

Grammar	*Can* (present ability)
	Adverb: *(not) very well*
Vocabulary	Verbs of ability
Function	Talk about things you can and
	can't do.

Get started

1 Can you name any charities? Do you ever raise money for charity?

Read

2 🔊 Listen and read along. Which do you think is the best charity event?

Comprehension

3 Answer the questions.

1 Where is the charity weekend?
2 When is it?
3 Which charity is it for?

Charity weekend

Every year Parkside Youth Club has a charity weekend for Friends of the Earth. This year it's on April 25 and 26. How can you help?

SPORTS EVENT

Can you run five miles? Ask your family and friends for 50 cents for every mile that you run. Maybe you can't run, but can you swim? Ask people for 50 cents for every lap that you swim.

TALENT SHOW

Can you sing or dance? Maybe you can play a musical instrument or juggle. Join our talent show and help to sell tickets.

ART SHOW

Some people can't sing or dance very well, but they can draw, paint, or take good photographs. Organize an art show at your school. Then sell the artwork.

FOOD STAND

Can you cook? Cook a dish for the food stand at the youth club and sell it to your friends.

Friends of the Earth

Solve it!

4 David gets $5 for the swimming event. How many laps does he swim?

Vocabulary: Verbs of ability

5a (2/27) Listen and repeat. Then match the activities below to the photos in Exercise 2.

Physical	Creative
_D_ swim	____ sing
____ run	____ play the guitar
Practical	____ paint
____ cook a meal	

b (2/28) Write each activity in the correct column. Then listen, check, and repeat.

- bake a cake • dance • draw • juggle
- ride a horse • sew on a button
- take photographs • type
- use a computer • use a washing machine

Physical	Creative	Practical
ride a horse		

Grammar

Can (present ability)	
Affirmative	**Negative**
I **can** sing.	I **can't** sing (very well).
Questions	**Short answers**
Can you sing?	Yes, I **can**.
	Yes, I **can**, but not very well.
	No, I **can't**.

☛ Go to page 134, Master your grammar.

Practice

6a In your notebook, write questions about the friends' abilities.

A: *Can David cook a meal?*   B: *No, he can't.*

	David	Laura	Carlos	Polly
cook a meal	✗	✓	✓	✗
bake a cake	✓	✗	✓	✓
use a computer	✓	✓	✓	✓
sew on a button	✗	✗	✓	✓

b PAIRS Ask a partner the questions in Exercise 6a.

Speak

7 Ask and answer questions about the activities in Exercise 5a.

A: *Can you sing?*   B: *Yes, I can. /No, I can't.*

Pronunciation: /æ/ c**a**n

8 Go to page 127.

Listen

9 (2/31) Listen. Then say what Suzy and Carlos can do.

Write

10 Choose a charity you like. On a piece of paper, write about what you can do to help that charity.

> **Extra practice**
> - Student Book, page 118, Lesson 7A
> - Language Builder: WB, page 50; GB, page 120
> - Student CD-ROM, Unit 7

Is there any salt?

Grammar	Count and noncount nouns: *some* and *any*
Vocabulary	Food
Function	Talk about food

Get started

1a Close your books. You have one minute. In your notebook, list all the food words you know.

b PAIRS Compare your list with a partner's. Whose list is longer?

Vocabulary: Food

2a  Listen and repeat.

18 apple ___ banana ___ bread ___ butter ___ carrot ___ cheese ___ chicken ___ cookie ___ egg ___ fish ___ grape ___ honey ___ meat ___ onion ___ orange ___ pasta ___ pepper ___ potato ___ rice ___ salt ___ sugar ___ tomato

b Match each item in the photo to a word in the box above.

Speak

3 PAIRS Talk with a partner about foods you like and foods you don't like.

I like cookies and bananas, but I don't like eggs.

Presentation

4 Listen and read along. Circle the words for food items.

Zach: What are you making, Polly?

Polly: I'm making a Spanish omelette.

Zach: Great! We have **some** eggs and **some** onions.

Polly: And I need **some** potatoes and **some** tomatoes, too.

Zach: OK. Here you go.

Polly: Thanks. Is there **any** salt?

Zach: Yes. There's **some** salt right here.

David: Oh, no!

Zach: What's the matter, David?

David: I have **some** apples and bananas for my fruit salad, but there aren't **any** oranges.

Zach: I'm afraid we don't have any oranges.

Polly: Wait! There are **some** oranges over there.

Carlos: Here's my dish, Zach. It's a pack of cookies. I can sell each cookie for 25 cents, and I'll have a free afternoon!

Zach: Not so fast, Carlos! What about cleaning up?

Phrases

 Listen and repeat.

• I'm afraid. • Not so fast! • What's the matter?

Comprehension

5 Write the ingredients for each dish.

Spanish omelette	Fruit salad
Eggs	Apples

Solve it!

6 Carlos pays $2.00 for a pack of cookies. There are 20 cookies in a pack. If Carlos sells all the cookies for 25 cents each, how much money does he make for charity?

Grammar

Count and noncount nouns

Count	Noncount
apples, oranges	salt, sugar
Affirmative	
There are **some** apples.	There's **some** salt.
Negative	
There aren't **any** oranges.	There isn't **any** sugar.
Questions	
Are there **any** grapes?	Is there **any** salt?

☞ Go to page 134, Master your grammar.

Practice

7 Copy the chart in your notebook and add more rows. Write the words from Exercise 2a in the chart.

Count	Noncount
carrot	bread

8 Complete the conversation with the correct form of *there is/are* and *some* or *any*.

Polly: What's in your pasta salad, Laura?

Laura: ¹ _There's some_ pasta, of course, and ² _____ onions and tomatoes, too.

Polly: ³ _____ cheese in it?

Laura: No, ⁴ _____ cheese, but ⁵ _____ eggs and apples.

Polly: ⁶ _____ nuts in it?

Laura: No. Don't worry. Oh look! ⁷ _____ chocolate cookies over there. Great!

Carlos: That's 25 cents, please. It's for charity!

Write

9 On a piece of paper, write a shopping list for a week's supply of food for yourself.

Shopping list
some eggs
some pasta

Extra practice
• Student Book, page 118, Lesson 7B
• Language Builder: WB, page 52; GB, page 120
• Student CD-ROM, Unit 7

Grammar	Imperatives
	Prepositions of place
Vocabulary	Places in town
Function	Ask for help

Get started

1 What places in your town or city do you know? In your notebook, list as many as you can.

Presentation

2 🎧 (2 35) Listen and read along. Does Polly have a map?

Laura: Don't move! I want a photo of you **in front of** the market. Say cheese. Great!

Polly: Let's go. I need some stamps for my postcards. Excuse me, is there a post office **near** here?

Boy: Yes, there's one on Burnside Street, **across from** the bank. It's **between** the bookstore and the drugstore.

Polly: Thanks.

Boy: No problem.

Laura: OK. Where's Burnside Street?

Polly: Don't ask me! I'm useless without a map!

Comprehension

3 Answer the questions.

1 What does Laura want to take a photo of?
2 What is Polly looking for? Why?
3 Do you think Polly and Laura find what they are looking for? Explain.

Grammar

Imperatives	
Affirmative	**Negative**
Say cheese.	Don't move!

☞ Go to page 134, Master your grammar.

Practice

4 **PAIRS** Give some classroom instructions to a partner. Use these verbs.

- listen • open • close • look • read
- ask • answer • talk • write

Vocabulary: Places in town

5a 🎧 (2 36) Listen and repeat.

- bank • bookstore • coffee shop • drugstore
- health club • park • parking lot • post office
- restaurant • supermarket • train station

b Match the words with the places in town.

1 stamp _post office_
2 book _____
3 pasta _____
4 train _____
5 money _____
6 car _____

7 medicine _____
8 swimming pool _____
9 trees _____
10 cup of coffee _____
11 milk _____

Grammar

Prepositions of place

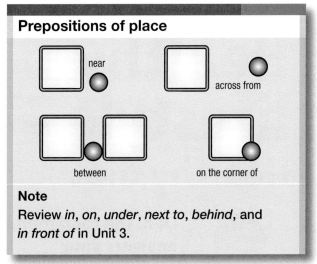

Note

Review *in*, *on*, *under*, *next to*, *behind*, and *in front of* in Unit 3.

☞ Go to page 134, Master your grammar.

Practice

6 Look at the map. Say where the places are.

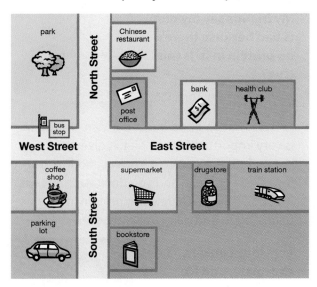

1 drugstore/train station
   The drugstore is next to the train station.
2 drugstore/supermarket + train station
3 supermarket/coffee shop
4 post office/North Street + East Street
5 Chinese restaurant/post office

Listen

7 ⟨2/37⟩ Look at the map in Exercise 6 and listen to four conversations. Write the missing place in each conversation. Then listen and check.

1 _____   3 _____
2 _____   4 _____

Use your English: Ask for help

8 ⟨2/38⟩ **PAIRS** Listen and repeat. Then practice the conversation.

A: Excuse me, is there a post office near here?
B: Yes, there's one on the corner of East Street and North Street.
A: Thanks.
B: You're welcome.

Ask where places are
• Excuse me, where's the train station?
• Excuse me, is there a drugstore near here?

Give a positive answer
• It's on East Street across from the health club.
• Yes, it is next to the train station.

Give a negative answer
• I'm sorry. I don't know. I'm not from here.

Say thank you
• Thanks so much./Thank you./Thanks.

Respond
• You're welcome.   • No problem.

---

9 Look at the map in Exercise 6 and ask questions about these places.

1 parking lot	3 bank	5 coffee shop
2 park	4 health club	6 bookstore

Write

10 What's your favorite place in your town or city? On a piece of paper, describe the place, its location, and why you like it.

 Extra practice
• **Student Book, page 119, Lesson 7C**
• **Language Builder: WB, page 54; GB, page 122**
• **Student CD-ROM, Unit 7**

Curriculum link: Biology

Get started

1 Which of these meals do you prefer?

Read

2 Read the web article. Do Marcel, Linda, and Isabel have healthy diets?

Learning strategy: Focus your reading

Before you read, look at the comprehension task. This will help you to focus on the information you need.

Comprehension

3 Read the web article again. Then complete the chart.

	Examples	Why they're important
Protein		
Carbohydrates		
Vitamins and minerals		

4 Use these food groups to label the pyramid on page 65. Write your answers in the colored boxes.

- dairy • fats and oils • fruit • grains
- protein • vegetables

File   Edit   View   Favorites

Healthy lifestyle – Healthy diet

Dan, the food man, answers your questions.

Q: I'm a vegetarian. My friends say my diet is bad because there's no protein in it. Is this true?

Marcel, 14, New York, U.S.

Dan: That's a good question, Marcel. Protein is very important in your diet. It gives you strength. There's protein in meat and fish, but if you're vegetarian and you don't eat meat or fish, don't worry. There's also protein in nuts, beans, eggs, and dairy (milk/cheese).

Q: I love cookies, chocolate, and ice cream. Is this a problem?

Linda, 16, Manchester, U.K.

Dan: I like those things too, Linda, but there are a lot of carbohydrates, sugar, and fat in sweet foods, so I only eat them once or twice a week. Carbohydrates aren't always bad for you. You need them for energy. But a lot of sugar and fat is bad for you. A healthy diet consists of protein, carbohydrates from grains and fruit, vitamins, minerals, and some fats.

MyPyramid

MyPyramid.gov

Fats and oils

Q: I know that fruit is important, but it's so boring! What can I do?

Isabel, 15, Mexico City, Mexico

Dan: It's true that fruit contains a lot of vitamins and minerals, but they are also in foods like vegetables, fish, and meat. Vitamins and minerals are important because they help your body to work properly. Try a smoothie. Put some bananas, apples, strawberries, and yogurt with some orange juice in a blender. It's great!

New words
- healthy • lifestyle • diet • vegetarian • strength
- nuts • carbohydrates • sweet • energy • contain
- properly • smoothie • yogurt • blender

5 PAIRS Complete the chart with foods you know.

A Healthy Lifestyle

Good for you	Not good for you

Listen

6 Mario is doing a project on sports diets for school. Listen to the interview and complete his notes.

	Food	Drink
• During training	*Carbohydrates,*	
• The night before the race		
• The morning of the race		
• During the race		

Speak

7a GROUPS Do a group survey. Ask what your group members usually have for breakfast.

b GROUPS Discuss: Does your group eat a healthy breakfast? What do you think is a healthy breakfast?

Write

8 On a piece of paper, write to Dan about your diet. Ask Dan what he thinks about it.

Hi, Dan,
I always have bread and butter for breakfast. I never drink milk. For lunch, I . . . For dinner, I . . . What do you think of my diet?

Comment by misha on July 29, 2011 @ 9:05 P.M.

CLIL PROJECT, page 140

What's he doing in California?

Grammar	Present continuous
Vocabulary	The weather
Function	Talk about the weather

Free time

8

Get started

1 Look out the window. What's the weather like?

Presentation

2 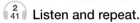 Listen and read along. Is it sunny in San Diego?

Polly: Come on, David! We**'re playing** soccer, and we need you as goalie!

David: Hang on a minute.

Carlos: What are you doing?

David: I**'m texting** my friend Luke. He's in California right now.

Polly: What**'s** he **doing** in California?

David: He**'s visiting** his aunt in San Diego.

Polly: How cool! What's the weather like in San Diego? Is it sunny? Is he at the beach?

David: No, he isn't. Believe it or not, it**'s raining** there right now, and he**'s sitting** in a coffee shop.

Phrases

2 41 Listen and repeat.

- Hang on a minute.
- How cool!
- Believe it or not.
- Come on!

Comprehension

3 Answer the questions.

1 Who asks David to play soccer? _____*Polly*_____
2 Who has a friend in California?_____
3 Who is in a coffee shop? _____
4 Who lives in San Diego? _____
5 Where is San Diego? _____

Grammar

Present continuous	
Affirmative	**Negative**
I'm **texting** my friend.	I'm **not calling**.
He's **visiting** his aunt.	He **isn't visiting** friends.
They're **playing** soccer.	They **aren't playing** golf.
Questions	**Short answers**
Are you **texting**?	Yes, I **am**./No, I'm **not**.
Is he **calling**?	Yes, he **is**./No, he **isn't**.
Are they **playing** soccer?	Yes, they **are**./No, they **aren't**.
What **are** you **reading**?	A mystery novel.
What **is** she **doing** now?	Texting a friend.

☛ Go to page 135, Master your grammar.

Practice

4 Fill in the blanks with the verbs in the box. Use the correct form of the present continuous.

> • do (x2) • lie • listen • make • play (x2) • watch

Laura: Hey, Polly. What ¹ _are_ you _doing_ tonight?

Polly: I ² _____ to some music.

Laura: Are your brothers with you?

Polly: No, they aren't. They ³ _____ soccer. What are you all doing?

Laura: We ⁴ _____ much. Dad ⁵ _____ dinner, and Sam ⁶ _____ on the floor.

Polly: ⁷ _____ he _____ video games?

Laura: No, he isn't. He ⁸ _____ TV.

Pronunciation: / ŋ / doi<u>ng</u>

5 Go to page 127.

Vocabulary: The weather

6 (2/44) Listen and repeat.

Speak

7 PAIRS Ask and answer about the photos.

A: *What's the weather like in Punta Cana?*

B: *It's . . .*

Punta Cana

Paris

Seattle

New York

Listen

8 (2/45) Listen to Diana and Steve. Then answer the questions in your notebook.

1 Where are they?   3 What's the weather like?

2 What month is it?   4 Why is the weather unusual?

Write

9 On a piece of paper, write about your favorite season. Tell what you like best about it.

> **Extra practice**
> • **Student Book, page 119, Lesson 8A**
> • **Language Builder: WB, page 58; GB, page 124**
> • **Student CD-ROM, Unit 8**

1 It's sunny. It's warm/hot.   2 It's foggy.   3 It's cloudy.   4 It's raining.   5 It's windy.   6 It's snowing. It's cold/freezing.

8B I'm playing basketball.

Grammar Simple present and present continuous
Vocabulary Sports
Functions Talk about sports

1 volleyball
2
3
4
5
6

Get started

1 Which sports are popular in your country?

Vocabulary: Sports

2a (2/46) Listen and repeat. Six sports are shown in the photos. Label them.

- basketball • baseball • cycling • football
- golf • gymnastics • skateboarding
- snowboarding • soccer • swimming • tennis
- volleyball • windsurfing

b Write the name of the sport next to the athlete who plays it. Use the words in the box above.

Tom Brady _football_   Serena Williams _____
Alex Rodriguez _____   Kaka _____
Lorena Ochoa _____   Lance Armstrong _____
Michael Phelps _____

Read

3 (2/47) Listen and read along. What are David's and Laura's favorite sports?

I'm playing basketball right now, but my favorite sport is soccer. I **play** soccer twice a week at school, and I watch it every Sunday. Laura **likes** tennis. She **takes** tennis lessons every Saturday. She**'s taking** a lesson now.

68

Grammar

Simple present

I **play** basketball twice a week.
Laura **takes** tennis lessons every Saturday.

Present continuous

I'm **playing** football right now.
She's **taking** a lesson now.

☞ Go to page 135, Master your grammar.

Practice

4 Complete with the simple present or present continuous form of the verbs.

BMX star's dream
by Simon Lane

Bicycle Motocross racing, BMX, is a boys' sport—or is it? Shanaze Reade is a young woman from Manchester, England. Shanaze [1] _____loves_____ (love) all sports, but her favorite is BMX cycling. She usually [2] _____ (train) near home, but today she [3] _____ (train) in London. When I find her, she [4] _____ (eat) a large plate of pasta, even though it's still morning. She [5] _____ (explain) that it gives her energy for her race in the afternoon. Shanaze usually [6] _____ (ride) outdoors, but at this event, she [7] _____ (ride) on an indoor track. She [8] _____ (train) in London today because she [9] _____ (want) to get a place in the next Olympic Games. Her dream? To win a gold medal!

 Solve it!

5 What time of day does Simon interview Shanaze?

Speak

6 GROUP Discuss: Which sports do you play? Which sports do you watch?

7 PAIRS Talk about the famous people in the photos. Use the words in the box.

1 David Beckham

2 Carrie Underwood

3 Nick Jonas

4 Nelly

- play golf • sing • act in a TV show • rap
- play baseball • play soccer • play basketball
- play football

A: *What does David Beckham usually do?*
B: *He plays soccer.*
A: *What's he doing in the photo?*
B: *He's playing golf.*

Write

8 On a piece of paper, write about a famous person from your country. Write what he or she usually does. Imagine what he or she is doing now.

Salma Hayek usually acts in movies. I think she's ...

> **Extra practice**
> - **Student Book, page 120, Lesson 8B.**
> - **Language Builder: WB, page 60; GB, page 125**
> - **Student CD-ROM, Unit 8**

8c I prefer being outside.

Grammar *Like, love, hate, prefer + -ing*
Vocabulary Free-time activities
Function Make and respond to suggestions

Get started

1 What do you do in your free time?

Read

2 Listen and read along. Where does David sometimes go with his dad?

Comprehension

3 Where are Polly, David, and Carlos? What are they doing?

I **don't like cooking** very much, but I **like having** barbecues outside with my friends. Sometimes I go to the beach with my dad and have a barbecue there. I **love going** to the beach!

I'm hanging out in the park with my friends today. I really **like skateboarding**. My brothers are watching a DVD, but I **prefer being** outside when the weather's nice.

I **love playing** video games. I'm playing *Pro World Tennis* right now. (I **hate playing** tennis in real life!) I also **like surfing** the Internet and **chatting** with my friends online.

Vocabulary: Free-time activities

4a Listen and repeat.

- swim/go swimming • shop/go shopping
- chat with your friends online • watch a DVD
- go to the beach • listen to music
- play video games • go to the movies
- surf the Internet • have a party
- hang out with friends • have a barbecue
- go to a concert • go skateboarding

b Copy the chart into your notebook and add more rows. Complete it with words from the box.

Indoors	Outdoors	Both
		go swimming

💡 Solve it!

5 Listen. What are the six people doing?

Grammar

Like, love, hate, prefer + -ing

I **like** hav**ing** barbecues.
He **loves** go**ing** to the beach.
She **doesn't like** cook**ing** very much.
They **hate** play**ing** tennis.
We **prefer** be**ing** outside (to stay**ing** inside).
Do you **like** skateboard**ing**?

☞ Go to page 135, Master your grammar.

Practice

6 In your notebook, write sentences using the cues.

1 you/like/surf the Internet?

   Do you like surfing the Internet?

2 I/love/chat with friends online

3 Monica/like/go shop?

4 I/prefer/skateboard/swim

5 the girls/like/listen to music?

6 Luis/love/hang out with friends

7 they/prefer/go to the beach/go shop?

7a PAIRS Write more activities in the chart. Rate the activities with checks (✓) and ✗s, as shown. Then ask a friend to rate them, too. Write your friend's ratings in the second column.

A: *Do you like going shopping?*   B: *No, I hate it.*

✓✓ = **love**   ✓ = **like**   ✗ = **don't like**   ✗✗ = **hate**

Activities	You	Partner
shopping		

b GROUPS Share your answers in small groups.

Use your English: Make and respond to suggestions

8 PAIRS Listen and repeat. Then practice the conversation.

Polly: Let's go skateboarding.

Laura: No, not today. How about watching a DVD?

Polly: I'm not sure. Why don't we go swimming?

Laura: OK. That's a good idea.

Make a suggestion

- Let's go skateboarding.
- Why don't we go swimming?
- How about watching a DVD?

Respond positively

- OK. That's a good idea.

Respond negatively

- I'm not sure.   • No, not today.

Write

9 On a piece of paper, write about your favorite free-time activities. Use the texts on page 70 as models.

⊳ Extra practice

- **Student Book, page 120, Lesson 8C**
- **Language Builder: WB, page 62; GB, page 126**
- **Student CD-ROM, Unit 8**

INTEGRATED **CONSOLIDATION** SKILLS

Values for living

Get started

1 What is a blog? Do you read any blogs? On which topics? Do you blog?

Read

2 Read Jessica's blog below. When are her exams?

○○○

HOME | **BLOGS** | GROUPS | VIDEO | CHAT

The big teen blog site

Blog about your life, your interests, and your issues!

About me
My name is Jessica Torres.
I'm 14. I LOVE playing volleyball, but I HATE taking exams!

me looking cool—not!

me at age three!

volleyball—my passion

Jessica's blog

January 15
Busy, busy, busy!
I'm sooo busy! I go to school, I play volleyball, I do my homework, and I help my mom at home. Today is Sunday, and I'm doing my homework!

March 16
It's only March, Mom!!!
Brrrrrrr. It's freezing today, and I HATE cold weather. My mom talks about my exams every day! It's only March, and the exams are in June!

April 1
SHOCKING NEWS!
Shocking news 1: I'm now captain of the school volleyball team!
Shocking news 2: Sam likes me! He's a boy at school. He's cool!
He wants to go to the movies with me next weekend.

May 5
Everyone is unhappy!
Sam isn't happy because I see him only once a week. My friends aren't happy because I don't see them at all. My mom isn't happy because I'm not studying for my exams . . .

June 15
Oh, no!
My exams are next week. I REALLY need to study for my exams this weekend, BUT . . .
1) There's a volleyball tournament all day on Saturday.
2) There's a barbecue at my friend's house on Saturday afternoon.
3) It's Sam's birthday on Sunday.
What do I do? IT'S DRIVING ME CRAZY!!!

New words
• teen • blog • site • interests • issues • passion • busy
• only • shocking • news • captain • see (spend time with)
• (un)happy • study • tournament

Comprehension

3 Circle the wrong information and correct the statements.

loves
1 Jessica (hates) playing volleyball.

2 She likes cold weather.

3 She thinks Sam is boring.

4 She sees Sam twice or three times a week.

5 She's studying hard for her exams.

Speak your mind!

> **Speaking tip: Don't rush**
>
> When you speak in English, take your time. Don't rush. Speak clearly.

4a **GROUPS** Read what Jessica's friends suggest on her blog. Then say who you think is right.

○ ○ ○

> Friends are really important. Why don't you go to the barbecue on Saturday and study for your exams on Sunday? **Jack**

> The volleyball tournament is important. Enjoy the tournament on Saturday and study for your exams on Sunday. **Chloe**

> Why don't you go out with Sam on his birthday? You can study for your exams on Saturday. **Daniel**

> *I think Chloe is right. Jessica is the captain of the volleyball team, and that's important.*

b Give Jessica another suggestion.

Hi, Jessica. Why don't you . . .

Listen

> **Learning strategy: Use pictures to predict**
>
> Before you listen, look at the picture that goes with the text. Pictures can give you clues about the subject matter of the text.
>
> Look at the picture below. Who is in the picture? What are they talking about?

5a [2 52] Listen to the conversation and answer the questions.

1 Who is Jessica talking to? _____
2 Why is she unhappy with Jessica? _____

b [2 52] Listen again and complete the sentences.

1 The teacher thinks Jessica is an _____ .
2 Jessica's test score isn't _____ .
3 In the future, Jessica wants to be _____ .
4 The teacher asks, "Why don't you _____ on Saturday and Sunday and _____ ?"

Write

6 On a piece of paper, write your own blog for a day. Use Jessica's blog to help you.

CLIL PROJECT, page 140

Grammar (40 points)

1 Complete the sentences with *can* or *can't . . . very well* and the verb in parentheses. (6 points)

Sarah ⁰ ___can't cook very well___ (cook ✗).

Tom ¹ _____ (play basketball ✓),

but he ² _____ (swim ✗).

Eve and Joe ³ _____ (dance ✗),

but they ⁴ _____ (sing ✓).

A: ⁵ _____ Sarah

_____ (play) the guitar?

B: Yes, she ⁶ _____ .

2 Complete with *some* or *any*. (5 points)

Laura: Look. Here's a recipe for Pasta Napolitana. We have ⁰ ___some___ onions, so that's OK.

David: Do we have ¹ _____ tomatoes?

Laura: Yes, we have ² _____ tomatoes. Now, do we have ³ _____ cream?

David: No, but we have ⁴ _____ milk.

Laura: Wait! We don't have ⁵ _____ pasta!

3 Complete the sentences with a preposition of location. (5 points)

My uncle lives ⁰ ___next___ ___to___ a school. He has a big yard ¹ b_____ his house and a small garden ² i____ f_____ o____ it. ³ B_____ the school is a field with a parking lot ⁴ n_____ t_____ it. There is a park ⁵ a_____ f_____ my uncle's house, too.

4 Complete the sentences with the correct form of the verb in parentheses. (5 points)

0 My brother loves ___watching___ sports on TV. (watch)

1 Do you like _____ early? (get up)

2 My sister hates _____ in the back of the car. (sit)

3 I don't like _____ letters by hand. (write)

4 We love _____ e-mails. (send)

5 I love _____ shopping. (go)

5 Circle the correct answer. (5 points)

0 My brother __ every day in the park.
   a) runs b) is running

1 Laura __ Johnny Depp.
   a) loves b) is loving

2 What __ there? Come here!
   a) do you do b) are you doing

3 Jack usually __ soccer after school.
   a) plays b) is playing

4 Camilla isn't here. She __ with her friend.
   a) texts b) is hanging out

5 Caroline is tired. She __ on the sofa.
   a) lies b) is lying

6 Complete the classroom instructions. Use these verbs to make affirmative or negative sentences. (6 points)

• c̶l̶o̶s̶e̶ • listen • look • open • speak
• talk • write

0 ___Close___ the door, please. It's time to start.

1 ✓ _____ at me.

2 ✓ _____ your books and turn to page 8.

3 ✓ _____ English, please.

4 Please ✗ _____ with a pen. Use a pencil.

5 ✓ _____ to this song.

6 ✗ Ssh! Please _____ .

7 Complete the e-mail with the correct form of the verbs in the box. (8 points)

• d̶o̶ • like • rain • read (x2) • shine • watch (x3)

Hi, Jake!
What are you ⁰ ___doing___ ? I ¹ _____ e-mail because it ² _____ outside.
My parents ³ _____ TV. They usually
⁴ _____ TV on Sundays. My sister
⁵ _____ a book. She ⁶ _____
mystery novels. She doesn't ⁷ _____
TV much. Oh, wow! The sun ⁸ _____ now.
I can go outside. Bye!
Jennifer

Vocabulary (40 points)

8 Write the words in the chart. (19 points)

> • basketball • carrot • cloudy • cold • dance
> • egg • fish • ~~foggy~~ • juggle • football
> • paint • potato • sing • soccer • sugar
> • sunny • swim • tennis • volleyball • windy

Weather	Sports	Food	Verbs of Ability
foggy			

9 Complete the sentences. (10 points)

0 You sit on a bench in a _____ *park* _____ .
1 You buy stamps at a _____ .
2 You eat out in a _____ .
3 You leave your car in a _____ .
4 You buy medicine at a _____ .
5 You buy food in a _____ .
6 You buy coffee in a _____ .
7 You buy books at a _____ .
8 You exercise at a _____ .
9 You catch a train at a _____ .
10 You get money at a _____ .

10 Complete the verb phrases with words from the box. (11 points)

> • barbecue • beach • book • DVD • movies
> • magazine • party • shopping • soccer
> • ~~swimming~~ • TV • video games

go	*swimming*	
go to the		
have a		
play		
read a		
watch (a)		

Use your English (20 points)

11 Circle the correct response. (10 points)

0 **A:** I have to go and meet Carlos. Bye, Mom.
  B: a) You're so fast! (b) Not so fast!) c) It's not fast!
  What about your homework!!
1 **A:** Oh, no! I don't believe it!
  B: a) I'm afraid.   b) What's the matter?
  c) What about you?
2 **A:** Thank you.
  B: a) No problem. b) I'm sorry. c) Excuse me.
3 **A:** Hurry up! We're late.
  B: a) Believe it or not. b) I'm afraid.
  c) Hang on a minute.
4 **A:** I have a new cell phone.
  B: a) It's lucky! b) How cool! c) Cool thing!
5 **A:** How are you doing at school?
  B: Really well, a) believe it or not.
  b) I don't believe. c) you believe.

12 Look at the jumbled conversation below. Number the lines in the correct order. (10 points)

Two friends are deciding what to do this afternoon.

_____ a) Good idea. The Java Bean coffee shop has
          free Internet. Do you know where it is?
_____ b) How about going to the movies?
_____ c) I don't know. Let's look up the movie times
          online.
_____ d) I'm not sure about swimming.
_*1*_ e) Let's go swimming this afternoon.
_____ f) Thanks!
_____ g) OK. So what do you want to do?
_____ h) The movies? OK. What's playing?
_____ i) Yes, there's one next to the post office.
_____ j) You're welcome.
_____ k) No. Excuse me, is there a Java Bean coffee
          shop near here?

SELF-CHECK	
Grammar	_____ /40
Vocabulary	_____ /40
Use your English	_____ /20
Total score	_____ /100

How was the concert?

Grammar	Simple past of *be*
Vocabulary	Past adverbial expressions
Function	Talk about past activities

Get started

1 Where were you last night?

Presentation

2 Listen and read along. How did Polly get cheap tickets?

David: Hi Polly! I like your Miley Cyrus bag. **Were** you at her concert last night?

Polly: Yes, I **was**—with my two brothers. She **was** great!

David: Where **were** your seats?

Polly: We **were** right in front of the stage.

Laura: How much **were** your tickets?

Polly: $30 each.

Laura: Wow! That price is amazing!

Polly: Yes, one of my brothers knows a guitarist in her band. He went to college with him.

David: You're so lucky. We **were** at the youth club party. It **was** really boring.

Comprehension

3 Answer the questions.

1 Where was Polly last night?
2 Who was Polly with?
3 Where were Polly's seats?
4 How much were the tickets?
5 How was the youth club party?

💡 Solve it!

4 What was the total cost of the tickets?

Pronunciation /h/ how

5 🎧 Go to page 127.

Vocabulary: Past adverbial expressions

6 Listen and repeat. Then number the expressions in order from last year to this morning. Imagine it is Wednesday.

__ yesterday	__ last night	__ this morning
__ last month	_1_ last year	__ last Friday
__ last weekend	__ last week	

Grammar

Simple past of *be* (singular and plural)

Affirmative	Negative
I **was** at the concert.	I **wasn't** at the movies.
She **was** at the concert.	She **wasn't** at the movies.
They **were** at the concert.	They **weren't** at the movies.

Questions	Short answers
Were you there, too?	Yes, I **was**./No, I **wasn't**.
Was she there, too?	Yes, she **was**./No, she **wasn't**.
Were they there, too?	Yes, they **were**./No, they **weren't**.
Where was she last night?	At a concert.
Where were her seats?	In front of the stage.

Note

at home **at** school **at** work **at** David's house
at the movies **at the** youth club

☞ Go to page 136, Master your grammar.

Practice

7 Complete with the correct form of the verb *be*.

Polly: Where ¹ _were_ you last Saturday? ² _____ you at the concert?

Carlos: No, I ³ _____ . There ⁴ _____ a family party at our house.

Polly: ⁵ _____ it fun? ⁶ _____ your cousins there?

Carlos: No, they ⁷ _____ . It ⁸ _____ a little boring. How ⁹ _____ the concert?

Polly: Great! Our seats ¹⁰ _____ good, and the concert ¹¹ _____ awesome!

8 In your notebook, use the cues to write conversations with *Where*.

1 you/yesterday?/
  at school? / ✗ /at a soccer game
  A: *Where were you yesterday?*
     Were you at school?
  B: *No, I wasn't. I was at a soccer game.*

2 David/at ten o'clock this morning?/
  at home?/ ✗ /at Carlos's house

3 you and your brothers/last night?/
  at the movies?/ ✗ /at a concert

4 your sister/last Thursday?/
  at home?/ ✗ /at work

Speak

9 PAIRS Ask and answer the questions in Exercise 8.

Write

10 Look at Polly's diary. Then complete her e-mail.

Monday	the pool + Laura
Tuesday	the movies + David
Wednesday	my uncle's house
Thursday	the youth club
Friday	Laura's house

●○○

Hi Kelly!
Last week I was really busy. On Monday I
¹ *was at the pool with Laura* . Then on
Tuesday I ² _____.
On Wednesday we ³ _____
_____. On Thursday I ⁴ _____
_____. Then last night I
⁵ _____. How was
your week?
Love, Polly

> **Extra practice**
> • Student Book, page 121, Lesson 9A
> • Language Builder: WB, page 66; GB, page 128
> • Student CD-ROM, Unit 9

Grammar	Simple past of regular verbs: affirmative and negative
	Prepositions of motion
Function	Talk about past events

1 Do you know anyone who walks in his or her sleep?

A bed in a high place!

One Friday night, 15-year-old Kate Nelson was asleep in her bed.

At one o'clock in the morning, she walked out of her house, across the street, and into a construction site. The security guards didn't notice her. Then she climbed up a 120-foot crane.

At two o'clock in the morning, a man walked past the site and noticed the girl on the crane. He called 911 and the fire department arrived immediately. A firefighter climbed up the crane and then realized that Kate was still asleep! He carried her down a big ladder. Three hours after leaving her house, she was back home again. When her parents asked her about her adventure, she didn't remember it.

Read

2 Listen to and read the newspaper article about the sleepwalker. How high was the crane?

Comprehension

3 Number the pictures on the right in the correct order.

Solve it!

4 What time was Kate back home?

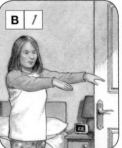

A | B | 1 | C | D | E

Grammar

Simple past of regular verbs: affirmative and negative

Affirmative

She **walked** out of the house.
The security guards **noticed** the girl.
He **carried** her down a ladder.

Negative

She **didn't walk** out of the house.
The security guards **didn't notice** the girl.
He **didn't carry** her down a ladder.

☞ Go to page 136, Master your grammar.

Practice

5 Complete the paragraph with verbs in the simple past form.

Yesterday morning I [1] ____*called*____
(call) my friend on my cell phone, but she
[2] _____ (not answer). I tried several
times, but I [3] _____ (not get) through.
Finally, I [4] _____ (walk) to her house.
I [5] _____ (knock) on the door and
[6] _____ (wait) for two or three minutes.
When she [7] _____ (not open) the door,
I suddenly [8] _____ (remember)—she
was on vacation in Bermuda!

Grammar

Prepositions of motion

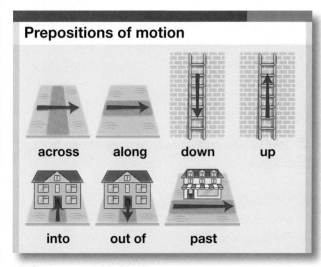

across   along   down   up

into   out of   past

☞ Go to page 136, Master your grammar.

Practice

6 Look at the pictures. Complete the story with the correct prepositions.

A Sleepwalker's Journey

The boy walked [1] ____*out of*____ the house,
[2] _____ the street, and [3] _____
some shops. He walked [4] _____ the
river for a mile, then [5] _____ a hill, and
[6] _____ a coffee shop. He ordered a cup
of hot chocolate. Then he walked [7] _____
the hill again and went back home. He was asleep
the whole time!

Speak

7 **PAIRS** Cover up the paragraph in Exercise 6.
Take turns saying what happened in each picture
above.

Write

8 On a piece of paper, write five sentences
about a dream you had.

> **Extra practice**
> • Student Book, page 121, Lesson 9B
> • Language Builder: WB, page 68; GB, page 129
> • Student CD-ROM, Unit 9

9c Where did you surf?

Grammar Simple past of regular verbs:
questions and short answers
Vocabulary Adjectives of feeling
Function Ask about problems

Get started

1 PAIRS Think of a time you disappointed someone. What happened?

Presentation

2 🎧 Listen and read along. What musical instrument does Carlos play?

Polly: What's the matter, Carlos?
Carlos: Nothing. I'm just a little upset. I failed my piano exam yesterday. Dad's really angry.
Polly: How often **did** you **practice**?
Did you **practice** a lot last week?
Carlos: No, I **didn't**. I surfed a lot.
Polly: You surfed? Where **did** you **surf**?
Carlos: At home. I surfed the Internet!

Comprehension

3 Answer the questions.

1 How does Carlos feel?
2 When was his piano exam?
3 Why was Carlos's dad angry?

Grammar

Simple past of regular verbs: questions and short answers
Yes/No questions
Did you **practice** last week?
Short answers
Yes, I **did**./No, I **didn't**.
Wh- questions
Where **did** you **surf**?

☞ Go to page 136, Master your grammar.

Practice

4 In your notebook, write questions and answers in the simple past.

1 A: David/play any sports last week? B: ✓
   A: What sports/play?
   B: basketball
   A: *Did David play any sports last week?*
   B: *Yes, he did.*
   A: *What sports did he play?*
   B: *He played basketball.*

2 A: Your sister/watch TV last night? B: ✗
   A: What/watch?
   B: a movie

3 A: You/call a friend last night? B: ✗
   A: Who/call?
   B: my brother

4 A: they/surf the Internet yesterday? B: ✓
   A: What websites/look at?
   B: Facebook.com

Speak

5 PAIRS Ask and answer two questions from Exercise 4.

A: *Did you play any sports last week?*
B: *No, I didn't. I played video games.*
A: *What game did you play?*
B: *The Invaders 12.0.*
A: *The new version? Cool!*

Read

6 Read the article. In your notebook, write questions asking the author about the missing information.

How old were you?

A shark attacked me!

Owen Williams

I was [1] [?] years old and I lived in [2] [?]. The shark attacked at [3] [?] o'clock in the morning. I was swimming with my friend Rachel. She noticed the shark in the water. She shouted [4] " [?] " but I didn't believe her. Then the shark attacked my [5] [?]. We quickly returned to the beach and I called [6] [?]. Luckily, Rachel and I were OK, and I still have the surfboard!

Listen

7 [3/08] Listen and answer the questions. Imagine you are Owen.

Q: *How old were you?*   A: *I was 14 years old.*

Vocabulary: Adjectives of feeling

8a [3/09] Listen and repeat.

> __ angry __ bored __ excited __ happy
> __ sad __ tired _1_ upset __ worried

b [3/10] Match the words to the sentences you hear.

Use your English: Ask about problems

9 [3/11] **PAIRS** Listen and repeat. Then practice the conversation.

A: What's the matter?
B: Nothing. I'm just a little tired.
A: Why are you tired?
B: Because I stayed up late last night.
A: That's too bad. Why don't you go to bed early tonight?

Ask if there is a problem	Respond
• What's the matter?	• Nothing. I'm fine.
• What's wrong?	• Nothing. I'm just a little upset/worried/sad.

Ask another question	Respond
• Why are you upset/ worried/sad?	• Because I failed my exam.

Offer sympathy or advice
• That's too bad./That's OK. Why don't you take it again?

10 Practice more conversations. Use the cues below.

1 A: wrong?   B: worried
   A: why/worried?   B: not finish/my homework last night
   A: do/it at lunchtime?
2 A: matter?   B: upset
   A: why/upset?   B: my friends/forgot my birthday

Write

11 Choose a situation from exercise 10. Write a conversation, then role-play it.

> **Extra practice**
> • **Student Book, page 122, Lesson 9C**
> • **Language Builder: WB, page 70; GB, page 129**
> • **Student CD-ROM, Unit 9**

INTEGRATED CONSOLIDATION SKILLS

Calling the world!

Cell phone facts

- In 1973, a man named Martin Cooper invented the cell phone. But the first cell phone didn't arrive in stores until 1983. It was big and heavy. It weighed four pounds.

- Today, three billion people around the world have a landline, while more than five billion people have a cell phone.

- In Latin America, 250 million people use cell phones; in India, 54 million; in the U.S., 230 million; in Africa, 310 million; and in China, 595 million!

- Cell phones are very popular in India, China, and many African countries because few people living in those places have landlines.

Get started

1 Number these inventions in order:
1 = not important, 4 = very important.

☐ the Internet   ☐ the cell phone
☐ the television ☐ the computer

Discuss: Which invention was the most important? Why?

Read

2 Read "Cell phone facts." Say why these numbers are important:

a) 1983   b) 595 million

New words

- invention • invent • heavy • weigh
- landline • popular • village • pay-as-you-go
- card • cheap • text messages • take photos
- alarm clock • addicted to

Comprehension

3 Read "Cell phone facts" again and answer the questions.

1 When did Martin Cooper invent the cell phone?
2 When did the first cell phone arrive in stores?
3 Why are cell phones popular in China and Africa?

Cell phones and you

There aren't any landlines in my village because it's in the country, but we have a cell phone. My whole family uses it. We buy pay-as-you-go cards. Some people in my village don't have a cell phone, but they use the village cell phone. It's cheap—you pay by the minute.

Jomo, 17, Kenya

My cell phone was a birthday present from my parents. I use it a lot. I make phone calls, send text messages, take photos, and surf the Internet. I even watch sports on it. It's also my alarm clock and my diary. My mom says I'm addicted to it.

Dan, 16, Chicago

Speak

4 GROUPS Talk about these questions.

1 Do students in your class have cell phones? What do they use them for?
2 What is your opinion of cell phones?

Listen

5 Listen and fill in the missing words.

The inventors of the first airplane were Orville and Wilbur [1] _____Wright_____. The first flight was in North Carolina, U.S., in [2] _____ . The flight lasted [3] _____ seconds, and the plane traveled [4] _____ feet. The first passenger flight was in [5] _____ , and the plane traveled at less than [6] _____ mile an hour.

Write

6a Compare and contrast how Jomo and Dan use their cell phones.

Jomo	Dan
1	1
2	2
3	3

b How do you use your cell phone? Write two sentences.

7 On a piece of paper, write a paragraph about the *Concorde*. Use the notes below. Be sure to check your work for errors in grammar, spelling, and punctuation.

The first supersonic airliner
Name: Concorde
The first flight: Toulouse, France
Date: March 2, 1969
Height: reached 9,842 ft
Duration of flight: 27 minutes
Speed: 300 mph (miles per hour)

CLIL PROJECT, page 140

83

I had so much fun!

Grammar Simple past of irregular verbs:
affirmative and negative
Vocabulary Transportation
Function Talk about types of transportation

Get started

1 How do you get to school every day?

Read

2  Listen and read along. What's a Zorb globe?

Comprehension

3 Write *T* for *true* or *F* for *false*. Underline the false information.

__F__ 1 The *tuk-tuk* has <u>four</u> wheels.

_____ 2 The Zorb globe is filled with air.

_____ 3 The ride in the Zorb globe was boring.

_____ 4 People brought goats and chickens on the chicken bus.

_____ 5 The chicken bus was cool and comfortable.

Solve it!

4 How much did the chicken bus ticket cost per person?

I took a ride in a Zorb globe! I sat inside the giant, air-filled ball as it rolled down a hill. I paid $37 for my ticket. It was expensive but worth it. I had so much fun!

I went on vacation to India with my family. We saw a funny little car called a *tuk-tuk* at the airport. It didn't have four wheels, it only had three. We took it to our hotel. The driver was in a hurry and drove very fast. We got to our hotel in ten minutes!

On my last trip to Guatemala with my mom, I went for a ride on a "chicken bus." The bus tickets cost us $8. People brought goats and chickens with them on the trip. The bus was crowded and hot, but I thought the experience was very interesting.

Grammar

Simple past of irregular verbs

Affirmative	Negative
It **had** three wheels.	It **didn't have** four wheels.
I **went** on vacation.	I **didn't go** on vacation.

☞ Go to page 137, Master your grammar.

Practice

5 Write sentences in the simple past.

1 I/not buy/a car. I/buy/a bike.
  I didn't buy a car. I bought a bike.

2 My parents/not go/to Paris. They/go/to Prague.
  _____

3 Polly/not have/lunch. She/have/a big breakfast.
  _____

4 My mom/not make/dinner. My dad/make/dinner.
  _____

6 In your notebook, rewrite the paragraph in the simple past.

> ### My school day
> I ¹ get up at 7:30 and ² take a shower. Then I ³ make some coffee, ⁴ sit in the kitchen, and ⁵ eat breakfast. At 8:15 I ⁶ put my books in my backpack and ⁷ run to school. On the way I usually ⁸ find some money in my pocket, so I ⁹ buy some chocolate. When I ¹⁰ get to school, I¹¹'m five minutes late!

Vocabulary: Transportation

7a 🎧 3/14 Listen and repeat. Then match the words with the pictures in the right column.

> _5_ bicycle/bike __ boat __ bus __ car
> __ truck __ motorcycle __ airplane/plane
> __ train

b Check (✓) how often you take each type of transportation.

Type of transportation	Often	Sometimes	Never
truck			
motorcycle			
car			
bus			
bike			
boat			
plane			
train			

Pronunciation: /ɑ/ c<u>ar</u>

8 🎧 Go to page 127.

Speak

9 PAIRS Brainstorm different types of transportation in your country. List them.

Write

10 Choose a type of transportation from your list in Exercise 9. On a piece of paper, write about it. Use the texts on page 84 as models.

> ❯ **Extra practice**
> • Student Book, page 122, Lesson 10A
> • Language Builder: WB, page 74; GB, page 132
> • Student CD-ROM, Unit 10

Grammar Simple past of irregular verbs: questions
Vocabulary Vacation activities
Function Talk about vacations

Get started

1 What's your favorite place for a vacation?

Presentation

2 Listen and read along. Circle the words and phrases that name vacation activities.

Dad: Hi, David! Welcome back! How was your vacation?

David: It was totally awesome, but it wasn't a vacation, Dad. It was a school trip.

Dad: OK, OK! **Did** you **have** a good time?

David: Yes, I **did**, thanks.

Laura: How was the youth hostel?

David: It was great!

Laura: What **did** you **do**? **Did** you **go** sightseeing?

David: Sightseeing? No way! We went hiking. We climbed halfway up Mount Hood. It was amazing.

Laura: **Did** you **buy** me a present?

David: No, I **didn't**. I spent my money on food. The food at the hostel wasn't a great part of the vacation.

Dad: Wait a minute! I thought you said it wasn't a vacation!

Phrases

3/18 Listen and repeat.
• Wait a minute! • No way!
• Welcome back! • totally awesome.

Comprehension

3 Put a check (✓) next to the good things and an ✗ next to the bad things about David's trip.

• the trip in general ( ) • climbing the mountain ( )
• the youth hostel ( ) • the food at the hostel ( )

Vocabulary: Vacation activities

4 3/19 Listen and repeat. Then write each activity in the correct column of the chart.

• go hiking/hike • go mountain biking
• go shopping/shop • go sightseeing/sightsee
• go skiing/ski • go swimming/swim
• go to a museum • go to the beach
• go windsurfing/windsurf

Town	Mountains	Ocean

Grammar

Simple past of irregular verbs: questions	
Questions	**Answers**
Did you have a good time?	Yes, I **did**. No, I **didn't**.
What **did they do**?	They **went** hiking.

☛ Go to page 137, Master your grammar.

Practice

5a Complete the postcard using the simple past of the verbs in parentheses.

> Dear Grandma,
> We ¹ _____ (have) a good time
> in Oregon. We ² _____ (do)
> a lot of different things. We
> ³ _____ (not go) to Portland.
> Instead, we ⁴ _____ (go) to
> the mountains, and we climbed halfway
> up Mount Hood. We ⁵ _____
> (get) home yesterday. Hope you're well.
> Love,
> David

b Use the cues to write questions and answers about David's trip in your notebook.

1 have/a good time?

   Did they have a good time? Yes, they did.

2 Where/go?

3 Which mountain/climb?

4 When/get home?

6a Write three more questions to ask a classmate about last weekend.

1 *What did you do last weekend?*

2 _____

3 _____

4 _____

b PAIRS Take turns asking each other your questions.

Use your English: Talk about vacations

7 GROUPS Read the conversation in Exercise 2 in groups of three.

Vacations in general
• How was your vacation?
● It was amazing/great/a little boring.

Place
• Where did you go? ● We went to Oregon.

Accommodations
• Where did you stay?
● We stayed in a hotel/hostel/at a campsite.

Weather and food
• What was the weather/food like?
● It was awesome/great/OK/not bad/awful.

Activities
• What did you do?
● We went to the beach/went sightseeing.

8a Imagine you're on vacation in Cancun. Take notes about the place, accommodations, weather, food, and activities.

Cancun

b PAIRS Now ask your partner about his or her vacation. Use the questions and answers in Exercise 7.

Write

9 You're on vacation in Cancun. On a piece of paper, write a text message to a friend about your trip. Use the information from Exercise 8 for ideas.

 Extra practice
  • Student Book, page 123, Lesson 10B
  • Language Builder: WB, page 76; GB, page 132
  • Student CD-ROM, Unit 10

Three days ago we saw the waterfalls.

Grammar	Simple past with *ago*
Vocabulary	Landforms
Function	Talk about a culture trip

Get started

1 How many countries in South America can you name in one minute?

Read

2 Listen to and read the article. How many countries does Rachel mention?

Open World trip
by Robert Sands

A

B

C

Quito
ECUADOR

Lima
PERU

BRAZIL

Rio de Janeiro

ARGENTINA

Buenos Aires

Three months ago Rachel Ford traveled across South America from Ecuador to Argentina. Why was her trip special? Rachel and the other 20 teenagers on the trip are disabled. Here is an excerpt from Rachel's diary.

July 5
Today we left Quito in Ecuador and traveled north to Lake Cuicocha. We went by boat across the lake past a big island. It wasn't easy to get my wheelchair on the boat.

July 10
Two days ago we took a train to Machu Picchu, the lost city of the Incas in Peru. It's high in the mountains!

July 16
Three days ago we saw the Iguazu waterfalls. They're between Argentina and Brazil. We got very wet! We arrived here in Rio de Janeiro in Brazil six hours ago.

July 27
Yesterday we went on a small plane from Rio to Buenos Aires, the capital of Argentina. Last night we saw some amazing tango dancers. I did a great wheelchair dance!

Comprehension

3a Write the name of each place.

A _____ B _____ C _____

b Answer the questions.

1 How many teenagers were there in the group?

_____

2 How did they travel
   a) across Lake Cuicocha? _____
   b) to Machu Picchu? _____
   c) to Buenos Aires? _____

 Solve it!

4 In what month did Robert Sands write the article "Open World trip"?

Vocabulary: Landforms

5a Listen and repeat. Then look at the photos on page 88. Write the letter of the photo next to the appropriate word. Two words do not match any of the photos.

___ coast ___ forest ___ hill ___ island ___ lake
___ mountain ___ ocean ___ river ___ sea
___ valley ___ waterfall

b Give an example for each of the following:

1 an island _____
2 an ocean _____
3 a sea _____
4 a river _____

Grammar

Simple past with *ago*

Three days ago we saw the Iguazu waterfalls.
We arrived in Brazil six hours ago.

☛ Go to page 137, Master your grammar.

Practice

6 In your notebook, answer these questions about Mike's trip. Use the simple past and *ago*.

> Mike is on a long rail trip in Europe.
> It is now 2:00 P.M. on Tuesday, May 25.

1 When did Mike buy the tickets for the trip?
   He bought the tickets four months ago.
2 When did Mike see the Colosseum in Rome?
3 When did Mike go on the London Eye?
4 When did Mike take the train to Paris?
5 When did Mike visit the Eiffel Tower?

> Tuesday, January 24:
> buy tickets for the trip to Europe
>
> Tuesday, March 28:
> see the Colosseum in Rome
>
> Tuesday, April 25:
> go on the London Eye
>
> Saturday, May 4:
> take the train to Paris
>
> Tuesday, May 25:
> 11 A.M. visit the Eiffel Tower

Speak

7 PAIRS Brainstorm places to go to on a culture trip. Pretend you went to one of these places. Ask and answer questions about what you did and saw in that place.

A: *Where did you go?* B: *We ...*

Write

8 Write a postcard to your family about your experience in the place you chose in Exercise 7.

> ▶ **Extra practice**
> • Student Book, page 123, Lesson 10C
> • Language Builder: WB, page 78; GB, page 133
> • Student CD-ROM, Unit 10

Heroes of the

Get Started

1 What explorers have you heard of?

Read

> **Learning strategy: Skim to get the general idea**
>
> When you read a text for the first time, read it quickly—or "skim" it—to get a general idea of what it's about.

2a Skim the text and match the main ideas (a–d) to the correct paragraph (1–4).

_____ a) Scott's journey back

_____ b) The race to the South Pole

_____ c) Scott's journey

_____ d) Amundsen's journey

b Now read the text.

Comprehension

3 Look at the map. Which explorer traveled on the orange route and which on the green route?

Green: _____

Orange: _____

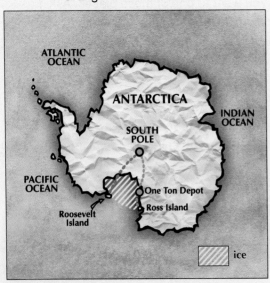

Scott

Amundsen

1 A hundred years ago, two explorers, Robert Falcon Scott from the U.K. and Roald Amundsen from Norway, started a race across Antarctica to the South Pole.

2 Amundsen started from Roosevelt Island on October 20, 1911. His team had good skiers and 50 dogs to pull their sleds. They moved fast across the ice and arrived at the South Pole on Friday, December 14.

3 Scott started from Ross Island on November 1, 1911. His team had horses, snowmobiles, and a few dogs. After a few days, the snowmobiles failed

Antarctic

Scott's team at the South Pole

and the animals were hungry and very cold. They traveled very slowly and didn't arrive until January 17, 1912. They were very disappointed when they found Amundsen's flag.

The return journey for Scott's men was a disaster. The weather was very bad, and they didn't have enough food. At the end of March, they died in their tents, only nine miles from One Ton Depot, where there was food.

New words
- hero • explorer • South Pole • skier • pull(ed)
- sled • move • fast • ice • horse • snowmobile
- fail(ed) • hungry • slowly • disappointed • flag
- return • journey • disaster • die • tent

4 Read the article again and use checks (✓) to complete the table.

Who . . .	Scott	Amundsen
1 had dogs?	✓	✓
2 had horses?		
3 had enough food?		
4 started at Ross Island?		
5 started in October 1911?		
6 arrived at the South Pole in January 1912?		

Speak

5 PAIRS Student A: You are a reporter in 1913. Ask Student B the questions below and add two more questions.
Student B: You are Roald Amundsen.

   A: *Where did you start your journey?*
   B: *We started from Roosevelt Island.*
1 How did you travel?
2 How long did your journey take?

Listen

6 🔊 3/22 Listen to two students talking about Marco Polo. Take notes.

1 Name of explorer	*Marco Polo*
2 Where did he go?	
3 Where did he start his journey?	
4 When did he start his journey?	
5 Who did he go with?	
6 How long did the journey take?	
7 How long did he stay in China?	
8 When did he arrive back in Italy?	

Write

7 On a piece of paper write about Marco Polo. Use your notes from Exercise 6 to help you.

Marco Polo was a famous Italian explorer. He traveled to China. He left Venice in 1271 and . . .

CLIL PROJECT, page 140

Grammar (40 Points)

1 Complete the conversation with *was, were, wasn't,* or *weren't.* **(8 points)**

A: How ⁰ _was_ Jack's party last night?

¹ _____ it good?

B: No, it ² _____ .

There ³ _____ many people there.

A: ⁴ _____ Emily and Jen there?

B: No, they ⁵ _____ .

Where ⁶ _____ you and Oscar?

A: We ⁷ _____ at the basketball game.

It ⁸ _____ great!

2 Use the cues to make questions and answers in the simple past. **(10 points)**

0 you/walk the dog today? (✓/this morning)

Did you walk the dog today?

Yes, I did. I walked him this morning.

1 Sarah/call this morning? (✗/yesterday)

2 What time/school end? (3 o'clock)

3 When/your cousins/arrive? (last night)

4 Daniel/practice the guitar today? (✓/after school)

5 you and Sue /like the movie?(✗/not like it at all)

3 Complete the sentences with *along, across, up, down, into, out of,* or *past.* **(6 points)**

0 Walk ____*past*____ the coffee shop and the bank is on your right.

1 I'm tired. I can't climb _____ that mountain.

2 He was very hot, so he jumped _____ the lake.

3 She walked _____ the street to the other side.

4 She walked _____ the river for ten minutes.

5 The firefighter carried the girl _____ the ladder.

6 He got _____ the shower and answered the phone.

4 Rewrite the paragraph in the simple past in your notebook. **(8 points)**

⁰ *Yesterday Tom got up at seven o'clock. He ...*

Every day Tom ⁰ *gets up* at seven o'clock.
He ¹ *goes* to the kitchen and ² *makes* a cup of tea. Then he ³ *takes* a shower. He ⁴ *doesn't have* breakfast. At eight o'clock he ⁵ *drives* to work. Before work he ⁶ *buys* some sandwiches and a newspaper and ⁷ *takes* them to work. Five minutes before work he ⁸ *does* the crossword puzzle!

5 Complete the letter with the correct word from the box. **(8 points)**

• at • by • Did • didn't (x2) • in
• ~~was~~ • wasn't • watched

Hi Jamie!

How ⁰ _was_ your weekend? ¹ _____ you go to the city? I ² _____ go out at all. I ³ _____ feeling well, so I stayed ⁴ _____ home. On Saturday night we ⁵ _____ have any food for dinner, so my mom ordered some pizzas. The pizzas arrived ⁶ _____ motorcycle ten minutes later! Cool or what! Then we ⁷ _____ a DVD of *High School Musical*. It isn't a new movie. It first came out ⁸ _____ 2006. It's really good.

See you later.

Robert

Vocabulary (40 points)

6 Complete the sentences with the correct adjectives of feeling. **(8 points)**

1 A: What's the matter? Are you ¹ a_____?

2 B: No, I'm not. I'm just ² u_____ because I can't do this homework.

3 I'm ³ b_____. There's nothing good on TV.

4 David is very ⁴ e_____. It's his birthday tomorrow.

5 I went to bed late last night so I'm a little ⁵ t_____.

6 The movie was very ⁶ s_____. It didn't have a ⁷ h_____ ending.

7 Where's Mom? She's very late. I'm a little ⁸ w_____.

7 Rearrange the letters to make landform words. (8 points)

0 mauntoni ___mountain___

1 refost _____   5 yalvel _____

2 virre _____   6 slinad _____

3 akle _____   7 canoe _____

4 esa _____   8 flatwarel _____

8 Solve the picture word puzzle. (6 points)

Across:

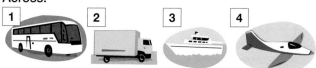

| 1 | 2 | 3 | 4 |

Down:

| 1 | 2 |

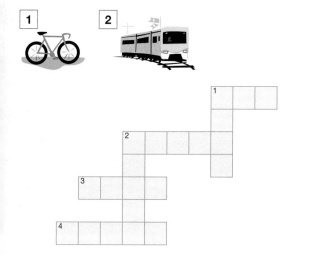

9 Write the vacation activities with *go*.
(18 points)

1 _____   2 _____   3 _____

4 _____   5 _____   6 _____

7 _____   8 _____   9 _____

Use your English (20 points)

10 Circle the correct response. (12 points)

0 A: Look, there's Dan. He got back yesterday.
   B: Hi, Dan. __
     a) You're welcome! (b) Welcome back!
     c) Welcome here!

1 A: How was your vacation?
   B: It was __
     a) really good fun. b) totally funny.
     c) totally awesome.

2 A: Oh, no! I failed my test!
   B: __
     a) Not worry. b) That's good. c) That's too bad.

3 A: We went home by bus.
   B: __ You said you walked home!
     a) Wait a minute. b) Only a minute.
     c) Wait some minutes.

4 A: Let's watch *American Idol*.
   B: __ I hate *American Idol*.
     a) That's OK. b) Welcome back! c) No way!

5 A: I'm upset.
   B: Why? __
     a) What is problem? b) What's the matter?
     c) What is matter?

6 A: I'm sorry I can't find your pen.
   B: __ I don't need it.
     a) Never mind. b) That's OK. c) That's bad.

11 Match the questions and answers to make a conversation. (8 points)

0 How was your vacation?   a) In a hotel outside San Juan.

1 Where did you go?   b) It was cloudy most of the time.

2 Where did you stay?   c) It was OK. But I was a little bored.

3 What was the weather like?   d) No, that was the problem. We went to museums every day.

4 Did you do any sightseeing?   e) We went to Puerto Rico.

SELF-CHECK	
Grammar	_____ /40
Vocabulary	_____ /40
Use your English	_____ /20
Total score	_____ /100

It's smaller and lighter.

Which cell phone?

Choices

11

Grammar Comparative and superlative of short adjectives

Vocabulary Short adjectives

Function Compare objects

	S50	XP3	Z5
Price:	$150	$90	$180
Size:	3.5x1.5x.5 in	4x1.5x.5 in	3x1.5x.5 in
Weight:	3.25 oz	4 oz	3 oz
Camera:	4 megapixels	3 megapixels	5 megapixels
Good photos:	4/5	3/5	5/5
Easy to use:	4/5	5/5	3/5

Get started

1 What's the most popular kind of cell phone in your school?

Presentation

2 (3/23) Listen and read along. Which cell phone does David like?

Carlos: Hey, David. Which of these three cell phones do you prefer?

David: Um, I'm not sure. The XP3 is the cheapest.

Carlos: Mmm. It's also the biggest and the heaviest of the three. The S50 is good. It's smaller and lighter than the XP3.

David: Yes, but the website says the XP3 is easier to use.

Carlos: I still prefer the S50. It's better than my old cell phone. It has two extra megapixels, and it's $40 cheaper!

David: The best phone is the Z5. It's the smallest and lightest of them all.

Carlos: Yes, but it's really expensive. Anyway, we don't have any money, so we can't buy any of them!

Comprehension

3 Rate the cell phones with one (✓), two (✓✓), or three checks (✓✓✓).

	S50	XP3	Z5
cheap	✓✓	✓✓✓	✓
small			
light			
good photos			
easy to use			

 Solve it!

4 How much was Carlos's old cell phone? How many megapixels did it have?

Speak

5 **PAIRS** Which of the three cell phones do you prefer? Why?

Vocabulary: Short adjectives

6 (3/24) Listen and repeat. Match the opposites.

bad	dirty
big	expensive
cheap	good
clean	small
cold	near
easy	light
far	hot
fast	old
heavy	short
long, tall	slow
new, young	hard

Grammar

Comparative and superlative of short adjectives

Adjective	Comparative	Superlative
small	smaller	smallest
Double consonant		
big	bigger	biggest
Words ending in -y		
heavy	heavier	heaviest
Irregular adjectives		
good	**better**	**best**
bad	**worse**	**worst**

The S50 is smaller than the XP3.
The XP3 is the cheapest phone.

☞ Go to page 138, Master your grammar.

Practice

7 Write the comparative and superlative forms.

Adjective	Comparative	Superlative
1 short	*shorter*	*shortest*
2 clean		
3 dirty		
4 hot		
5 bad		
6 easy		

Practice

8 Compare the cars. In your notebook, write a sentence for each adjective.

1 old 2 fast 3 slow 4 cheap 5 small

1 The Mono is older than the Ditsu, but the Posh is the oldest of the three cars.

SECOND-HAND CARS FOR SALE

1 The Mono	**2 The Posh**	**3 The Ditsu**
Year: 2002	Year: 2000	Year: 2008
Top speed: 65 mph	Top speed: 150 mph	Top speed: 120 mph
Price $1,000	Price $5,000	Price: $13,000

Listen

9 (3/25) Listen. Write two reasons why Greg's new bike is better than his old one.

1 _____

2 _____

Write

10 Think of two cell phones, video games, or other objects. On a piece of paper, compare the two items you chose.

> **Extra practice**
> • Student Book, page 123, Lesson 11A
> • Language Builder: WB, page 82; GB, page 136
> • Student CD-ROM, Unit 11

11B He's more famous than . . .

Grammar	Comparative and superlative of long adjectives
Vocabulary	Adjectives of quality
Function	Give your opinion

Get started

1 Who do you think is the most attractive actor or actress in the world?

Vocabulary: Adjectives of quality

2a 🎧 (3/26) Listen and repeat.

- attractive • beautiful • boring • dangerous
- difficult • exciting • famous • important
- interesting • scary • talented • useful

b Write each adjective from Exercise 2a in the appropriate column.

Positive	Negative

Read

3 Read the survey. What is the title of the magazine?

Comprehension

4 Cover the survey. Write down the choices you remember for each category.

1 the most talented athlete

_____

2 the most beautiful actress

_____

3 the most attractive actor

_____

4 the most useful gadget

_____

5 the most important invention

_____

Megan Fox

Cristiano Ronaldo

Survey: simpl

Young Style magazine wants your opinions. Is Maria Sharapova **more talented than** Cristiano Ronaldo? Is the cell phone **more useful than** the MP3 player? Who are **the biggest** stars, and what is **the best** gadget in the world today? Vote now!

1 Who is the most talented athlete?
a) Apolo Ohno   b) Cristiano Ronaldo
c) Maria Sharapova   d) other: _____

2 Who is the most beautiful actress?
a) Megan Fox   b) Zoe Saldana
c) Keira Knightley   d) other: _____

3 Who is the most attractive actor?
a) Gael Garcia Bernal   b) Robert Pattinson
c) Shia LaBeouf   d) other: _____

4 What is the most useful gadget?
a) the MP3 player   b) the cell phone
c) the digital camera   d) other: _____

5 What is the most important invention of the last 100 years?
a) the personal computer   b) the Internet
c) the television   d) other: _____

Gael Garcia Bernal

e best!

Grammar

Comparative and superlative of long adjectives

Comparative

Ronaldo is **more famous than** Ohno.
Megan Fox is **more beautiful than** Keira Knightley.

Superlative

Beckham is **the most famous** soccer player in the world.
Robert Pattinson is **the most attractive** actor in the world.

☞ Go to page 138, Master your grammar.

Practice

5 In your notebook, write sentences using the cues.

1 Lionel Messi/talented/soccer player in the world
   Lionel Messi is the most talented soccer player in the world.
2 The Harry Potter books/exciting/the movies
3 The Internet/useful/books
4 Beyoncé/famous/Shakira
5 A computer/expensive/a cell phone
6 The plane/important/invention of the 20th century

Lionel Messi

Speak

6 **PAIRS** Talk about the survey questions.

A: *Who's the most talented athlete?*
B: *I think it's Maria Sharapova.*
A: *Really? I disagree. I think Cristiano Ronaldo is more talented than Sharapova.*

Write

7 Choose a category from the survey in Exercise 3. On a piece of paper, write a paragraph explaining your choice.

   I think the most useful gadget ever invented is the cell phone! With my cell phone, I can . . .

> **Extra practice**
> • Student Book, page 124, Lesson 11B
> • Language Builder: WB, page 84; GB, page 136
> • Student CD-ROM, Unit 11

11c I like the green ones.

Grammar	*Which* +indefinite pronoun: *one/ones*
Vocabulary	Clothes
Function	Shopping for clothes

Get started

1 Where do you shop for clothes?

Vocabulary: Clothes

2a (3/27) Listen and repeat. Which items can you find in the photo?

> • baseball cap • belt • boots • cardigan
> • coat • dress • hat • hoodie • jacket • jeans
> • pants • sandals • shirt • shoes • shorts
> • skirt • sneakers • socks • sweater
> • sweatshirt • T-shirt • tights • top

b Copy the chart in your notebook. Write each word in the correct column according to how often you wear the item.

Every day	Sometimes	Never
jeans		

Presentation

3 (3/28) Listen and read. What does David buy?

David: Excuse me, do you have any cargo pants?
Assistant: Yes, there are some here.
David: I like the green **ones**. May I try these on?
Assistant: Sure. The fitting room is over there.

*   *   *

Assistant: Do they fit?
David: No. They're too big. Do you have them in a smaller size?
Assistant: Yes, here's a size 28. Try these.

*   *   *

David: These are fine. How much are they?
Assistant: They're $40.
David: OK. I'll take them. I need a belt, too. How about that **one**, Laura? What do you think?
Laura: Which **one**?
David: The brown **one**.
Laura: New pants, a new belt! Do you have a new girlfriend?

Comprehension

4 Answer *T* for true, *F* for false, or *NEI* for not enough information.

_____ 1 David wants a new pair of jeans.
_____ 2 David tries on two pairs of pants.
_____ 3 David wears size 30 pants.
_____ 4 The pants cost $80.
_____ 5 Laura likes the brown belt.

Grammar

> ### *Which* + indefinite pronoun: *one/ones*
>
> I like that belt. Which **one**?
> The brown **one**. This/That **one**.
>
> I like those jeans. Which **ones**?
> The dark blue **ones**.

☞ Go to page 138, Master your grammar.

Practice

5 Complete the sentences with *one* or *ones*.

1 I need a new dress. I don't like my old

_____.

2 I have lots of shoes. The gray _____ are
my favorite pair.

3 **A:** What do you think of the boots?
B: Which _____?

4 **A:** Where's my T-shirt?
B: The blue or the white _____?

5 Those are cool socks! I really like the red

_____.

Pronunciation: /ʃ/ shirt

6 🎧 Go to page 127.

Speak

7 **PAIRS** Ask to try on clothes. Use the words
one or *ones*. Use the photo below for ideas.

A: *May I try that shirt on?*
B: *Which one?*
A: *The blue one.*

Note: *too + adjective*

These jeans are OK.   These jeans are **too long**.

Use your English: Shopping for clothes

8a 🔊 3/31 Listen and repeat David's conversation
about the cargo pants in Exercise 3.

Ask to try on
- Excuse me, do you have any white/black
  T-shirts/jeans?
- Yes, there are some here.
- May I try this one/these on?
- Sure. The fitting room is over there.

Comment
- It's/They're too small/big.   • Try this/these.

Ask the price
- How much is it/are they?   • It's/They're $40.

Decide
- This one's/these are fine/perfect.
- I'll take it/them.
- No, I don't like it/them. Thanks anyway.

b **PAIRS** You're shopping for clothes. Your
partner is a store clerk. Role-play a conversation
at a clothes store.

Write

9 Your best friend is having a birthday party on
Saturday night and is going to invite someone you
really like. You want to look your best! On a piece
of paper, describe what you will wear.

> **Extra practice**
> • Student Book, page 124, Lesson 11C
> • Language Builder: WB, page 86; GB, page 138
> • Student CD-ROM, Unit 11

11D A problem at school

Values for living

Get started

1 What's a bully? Are there bullies in your school?

Read

2 Read the text. Why did William move to a new school?

New school – new problems

William is 14 years old. From the age of 11 to 13, he went to a junior high school near Portland. He liked the school, and he was happy there. He was smart, and he loved math and computers. He started an afterschool computer club, and he had some close friends. Then his father got a new job in Seattle, and William transferred to a new school.

The new school was bigger, and he was the youngest and smallest boy in his class. Some of the older boys laughed at him and called him names. Their favorite name for William was "geek" because he liked computers and was good at math. They teased him about his glasses. He had one friend in his class named Alex, but Alex never helped him. He was too scared. One day before school, Chad, one of the older boys, said, "William, give me your math homework. I want to copy it before the class."

William said nothing and gave his homework to Chad, but he was very upset. He didn't know what to do.

Comprehension

3 Read the article again. Check (✓) *New school* or *Old school*.

	New school	Old school
1 William went there for three years.		✓
2 Other students teased him.		
3 He started a computer club.		
4 He liked the school.		
5 His friend didn't help.		
6 He was unhappy at the school.		

Speak your mind!

4 Look at some advice for William. Number the advice from the best (1) to the worst (5). Then compare your answers with a partner.

A: *I think Jan's advice is the best.*
B: *I don't agree. I think Helene's advice is better than Jan's.*

- Don't give the boys your homework. Talk to your friends. They can help you.
  (Claudia, 15, Bogotá)

- Give them your homework. They're bigger than you.
  (Jan, 15, New York)

- Tell your parents and your teachers about the bullying.
  (Thomas, 14, Miami)

- Buy some cooler glasses and don't talk about computers.
  (Ana, 15, La Paz)

- Take karate lessons or go to a gym and get stronger!
  (Helene, 14, Paris)

Listen

Learning strategy: Listen for general meaning

The first time you listen, try to understand the general meaning of what is being said. Don't worry if you don't understand details.

5a 3/32 Listen. Which advice from Exercise 4 does William take?

b Listen again and answer the questions.

1 Who did William talk to? _____
2 What do the boys laugh at? _____
3 One of Mr. Saville's students had the same problem last year. What did Mr. Saville do? _____

Write

6 You are William. It's one month later. On a piece of paper, write an e-mail to your friend Mike. Write about your new school.

Hi Mike,

How are things? I started my new school last month. I wasn't happy at first. Some boys in my class. . . . And one day, one of the boys. . . .

William

CLIL PROJECT, page 140

Alex (William's friend at the new school)

"I want to help William, but the boys are bigger and stronger than I am. What if they start to bully _me_?"

Chad

"Why is William upset? I was just kidding around!"

New words
- smart • afterschool (adj)
- transferred • laugh(ed) at
- call(ed) (him) names
- "geek" • tease(d) • glasses
- scared • give (gave) • copy
- strong • bully

I'm going to record an album.

Grammar	*Be + going to* for future plans and intentions
Vocabulary	Types of music
Function	Talk about future plans

Get started

1 **PAIRS** Work with a partner. In one minute, list all the types of music that you can think of. Then compare your lists.

Read

2 🎧 ³₃₃ Listen and read along. Where is Adriana from?

Comprehension

3 Write *T* for true or *F* for false.

_____ 1 Adriana won the competition.

_____ 2 Adriana's song is rap.

_____ 3 Adriana wrote the song "Living Now."

_____ 4 Adriana is going to stay in school.

_____ 5 Adriana is excited about recording an album.

Adriana is the winner of the *American Dream* competition. This year, more than a thousand people entered. The songs included pop, rap, reggae, and rock. We talked to Adriana after the show.

Congratulations, Adriana. What are you going to do now?
I'm going to celebrate tonight with the other finalists. We're going to go out to dinner. Then I'm going to see the Hollywood Walk of Fame tomorrow.

Tell us about your song, "Living Now."
It's a pop song. My sister, Lisa, wrote it, and my brother, Victor, produced it.

Are your brother and sister here in Los Angeles today?
No, they aren't, but I'm going to see them next week when I go back home to Austin. They're going to have a big party for me.

What are your plans for the future?
I'm not going to leave school yet. My sister is going to write some more songs for me, and I'm going to record an album with my brother. I can't wait!

Grammar

Be + *going to* for future plans and intentions

Affirmative

I'm going to celebrate tonight.

Questions

What are you going to do?
Are you going to record an album?

Negative

I'm not going to leave school.

Answers

I'm going to record an album.
Yes, I am./No, I'm not.

Note: Future time phrases

- tonight • tomorrow • on Saturday (night)
- next week/month/year/summer

☛ Go to page 139, Master your grammar.

Practice

4 Complete the article about Mei-Li with *going to* and the correct form of the verb.

Next summer, Mei-Li ¹_____
(learn) guitar in Spain. She doesn't speak
Spanish very well, so she ²_____
(take) Spanish lessons, too. Her parents
³_____ (not be) with her. "I
⁴_____ (not see) my parents
for three months. I ⁵_____
(live) with a Spanish family," says Mei-Li. Next
year, a Spanish student ⁶_____
(come) to stay in New York with Mei-Li's family.

5 Write questions using the cues.

1 do/after school today?

What are you going to do afer school today?

2 have/for dinner this evening?

_____

3 watch/on TV tonight?

_____

4 wear/tomorrow?

_____

Speak

6 **PAIRS** Ask and answer the questions
in Exercise 5 with a partner.

Vocabulary: Types of music

7a 🎵 ³⁄₃₄ Listen and repeat.

- classical • country • folk • heavy metal • hip-hop
- jazz • pop • R & B • rap • reggae • reggaeton
- rock • salsa • soul • techno

b What's your favorite type of music?

Pronunciation: /dʒ/ jazz

8 🎧 Go to page 127.

Listen

9 🎵 ³⁄₃₇ Listen. Complete the chart.

Musician	Country	Type of music
Mac	*Jamaica*	
Ilhan		
Gabriela		

Write

10 You won a singing competition. On a
piece of paper, write about your plans after the
competition. Use Adriana's interview for ideas.

> **Extra practice**
> - Student Book, page 125, Lesson 12A
> - Language Builder: WB, page 90; GB, page 140
> - Student CD-ROM, Unit 12

Whose idea was that?

Grammar	Possessive pronouns
	Question word: *Whose ...?*
Vocabulary	Adverbs
Function	Talk about possessions

Get started

1 Do you have a special talent? What is it?

Presentation

2 (3/38) Listen and read along. What is Carlos worried about?

Zach: What are you guys going to do for the talent show next week?

Carlos: We're going to perform a rap version of *Romeo and Juliet*. I'm the director.

Zach: A rap version of *Romeo and Juliet*! Interesting! **Whose** idea was that?

Carlos: It was **mine**.

Zach: Great idea! Good luck!

Carlos: Thanks.

Carlos, Laura, David, and Polly are rehearsing for the talent show.

Carlos: OK, guys. Can we start quickly, please?

David: Sure. No problem.

Laura: Hey, guys! **Whose** dress is this? I found it on the floor. David, is it **yours**?

David: Very funny. No, it's not. It's **Polly's**.

Carlos: Don't worry about the dress. Let's start! David, rap your lines clearly and loudly. Laura, music please!

David: *What light through yonder window breaks? It is the east, and Juliet is the sun.*

Carlos: Stop, stop! Oh, man! We really need to work hard this week!

 Solve it!

3 Which Shakespeare characters do Polly and David play?

Phrases

(3/39) **Listen and repeat.**

- Let's start! • Good luck!
- No problem.

Comprehension

4 Answer these questions.

1 What's going to happen next week?

2 What's interesting and unique about Carlos's idea for *Romeo and Juliet*?

3 Did David deliver his lines well? How did you know?

Grammar

Possessive pronouns

Possessive adjectives	Possessive pronouns
my	mine
your	yours
his	his
her	hers
our	ours
their	theirs

Question word: *Whose . . . ?* **Possessive** *'s*

Whose dress is this? It's **Polly's**.

☛ Go to page 139, Master your grammar.

Practice

5 In your notebook, write questions and answers using the cues. Use *Whose?*, possessive *'s*, and possessive pronouns.

1 A: DVD?/Kate? B: my DVD

Whose DVD is that? Is it Kate's?
No, it isn't. It's mine.

2 A: books?/your parents? B: our books
3 A: orange juice?/Paul? B: your orange juice
4 A: house?/Emma? B: their house

Speak

6 PAIRS Take turns. Point to three things your classmates have. Ask *whose* questions. Use possessive pronouns.

A: *Whose backpack is that?*
B: *It's hers.*

Vocabulary: Adverbs

7 🔊 ³⁄₄₀ Listen and repeat. Then underline all the adverbs in the conversation in Exercise 2.

	Adjective	Adverb	Adjective	Adverb
Regular adverbs	angry	angrily	noisy	noisily
	bad	badly	patient	patiently
	careful	carefully	polite	politely
	careless	carelessly	quick	quickly
	clear	clearly	quiet	quietly
	loud	loudly	slow	slowly
Irregular adverbs	early	early	hard	hard
	fast	fast	late	late
	good	well		

8 Change the adjectives to adverbs in the quiz. Then take the quiz.

How patient are you?

1 You have your favorite food for lunch. Do you eat it

a) (fast) *fast* or   b) (slow) *slowly* ?

2 A student in your class asks you the same question three times. Do you answer

a) (polite) _____ or b) (angry) _____ ?

3 You are late for school and you are on your bicycle. Do you ride it

a) (quick) _____ and (careless) _____ or
b) (slow) _____ and (careful) _____ ?

4 You are talking to someone who doesn't speak your language very well. Do you speak

a) (natural) _____ and (fast) _____ or
b) (slow) _____ and (clear) _____ ?

Quiz answers: Mostly a) You live a fast life
Mostly b) You live a slower life.

Write

9 On a piece of paper, write a paragraph comparing yourself with another person. Use adjectives and adverbs.

> ## Extra practice
> • Student Book, page 125, Lesson 12B
> • Language Builder: WB, page 92; GB, page 141
> • Student CD-ROM, Unit 12

I want to see the video.

Grammar	*Want* + infinitive
	Want + object pronoun + infinitive
Function	Invite, accept, and refuse

Get started

1 What do you want to do today?

Presentation

2  Listen and read along. Does Carlos go to Laura's house?

Zach: Great job, everyone! You came in second place! That's awesome!

Carlos: Yeah, we rock! Can you take our photo, Zach?

Polly: Oh no. I **don't want to** be in the photo. I hate photos.

Carlos: Oh, come on, Polly! I **want you** and David **to** stand there, like Romeo and Juliet.

Zach: I have a video of your rap. Do you **want to** borrow it?

Laura: Yes, please! Hey guys, would you like to come to our house and watch the video?

Polly: That would be great! What about you, Carlos?

Carlos: I'd like to, but I can't. My dad **wants me to** help him with his new computer.

Laura: Oh, come on, Carlos!

Carlos: All right. But just for an hour.

David: Cool! Let's go. I **want to** see the video.

Comprehension

3 Answer the questions.

1 How did the friends do in the talent show?

2 What is on Zach's video?

3 What are the friends going to do now?

4 What is Carlos going to do after that?

Grammar

> ### *Want* + infinitive
>
> I **want to see** the video.
> I **don't want to be** in the photo.
>
> ### *Want* + object pronoun + infinitive
>
> I **want you** and **him to stand** there.
> He **wants me to help him** with his computer.

☞ Go to page 139, Master your grammar.

Practice

4 In your notebook, write sentences with *want to*.

1 Laura/not learn German/learn Spanish
Laura doesn't want to learn German.
She wants to learn Spanish.

2 Polly/not listen to classical music/listen to rap

3 Carlos/not be in the play/be the director

4 I/not study music/study English

5 David/not do his homework/watch TV

1 Can you open the window, please?

2 Can you do this again, please?

3 Can you buy some milk, please?

4 Can you clean your room, please?

5 Can you wash the dishes, please?

5 PAIRS Look at the pictures. Take turns saying sentences with *want to*.

1 She wants him to open the window.

Use your English: Invite, accept, and refuse

6 3/42 GROUPS Listen and repeat. Then practice the conversation.

A: Would you like to come to a soccer game? My dad has some free tickets.
B: When is it?
A: It's on Saturday, July 26, at Quest Field.
B: I'd love to. Thanks! What time does it start?
A: It starts at three o'clock. What about you, Tom?
C: I'm sorry, I can't.

Invite
• Would you like to come to a soccer game?

Ask when and where
• When is it?
• It's on Saturday, July 26.
• Where is it?
• It's at Quest Field.
• What time does it start?
• At three o'clock.

Accept
• I'd love to. Thanks!
• That would be great. Thanks!

Refuse
• I'm sorry, I can't. • I'd like to, but I can't.

7 PAIRS Invite your partner to these events. He or she must accept two events and refuse the other two.

Paramount Theater
RENT
Wednesday,
July 14, 7 P.M.

Basketball playoffs
Madison Square
Garden
Saturday,
May 5, 3 P.M.

RANGO
Ridgeway
Movie Theater
SUNDAY
MARCH 13
6:30 P.M.

Talent Contest
Parkside Youth Club
Friday, August 15, 5 P.M.

Write

8 On a piece of paper, write text messages inviting friends to four different events.

> **Extra practice**
> • Student Book, page 125, Lesson 12C
> • Language Builder: WB, page 94; GB, page 142
> • Student CD-ROM, Unit 12

12D Crazy festivals

Get started

1 What is the craziest festival you've seen or heard of? Describe it.

Read

2 Read about these crazy festivals. As you read, take notes.

Strange festivals

Everyone knows about Christmas, Easter, and Halloween.
But have you heard of these festivals?

The Maldon Mud Race

On the last week of every year, about 200 people do a 500-meter mud race. This race is across the River Blackwater in the town of Maldon in Essex, England. First, the participants put on funny clothes. Next, they swim through freezing water. Then they run (or crawl) through 200 meters of mud. Finally, they run back to where they started. The race takes about five minutes. What special prize do the participants get? A cold shower!

La Tomatina

"La Tomatina" is a big tomato fight that happens every year in Buñol, Spain, on the last Wednesday in August. First, trucks full of overripe tomatoes come into the center of town. Then at exactly 11:00 A.M., everyone grabs tomatoes, and the throwing begins. In just minutes, the town and everyone in it is bright red. The fight lasts until 1:00 P.M. Finally, all the tired but happy people start the big job of cleaning up the mess.

New words
- strange • festival • mud • put on (clothes) • fancy • through • crawl • prize
- participants • fight • overripe • center of town • exactly • grabs • throw • begin • mess

Comprehension

3 Complete the chart. Use your notes from Exercise 2.

	The Maldon Mud Race	La Tomatina
1 Date	*last week of the year*	
2 Location		
3 Activity		
4 Time		
5 Prize		

 Solve it!

4 On what date is La Tomatina going to be next year? Use a calendar.

Listen

5 ³⁄₄₃ Listen. Write the steps for the frog jump competition.

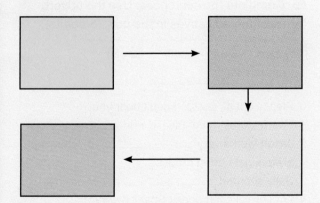

Speak

6 PAIRS Talk about a crazy or unusual event in your home country.

1 What is the name of the festival?
2 When is it?
3 What do people do? Do they wear any special clothes or eat any special food?

Write

Writing tip: Organize your ideas

To organize your ideas and show the order of events in your writing, use sequence words such as *first*, *next*, *then*, and *finally*.

First, the participants put on fancy clothes.

Next, they swim through freezing water.

Then they run through the mud.

Finally, they run back to where they started.

7 Read Richard's e-mail and complete it with the correct sequence words.

⊖ ○ ○

Hi David,

Guess what I did during my trip to England? I ran in a mud race! ¹_____, we put on crazy clothes. ²_____, we swam in a river. ³_____ we crawled through the mud. It was freezing! ⁴_____, some people took cold showers! Not me! My shower was long and hot.

See you soon!
Richard

8 In your notebook, write three sentences for each set of cues. Use sequence words.

1 get up and eat breakfast/go for a long walk/eat a big lunch

   First, we got up and ate breakfast. Next we went for a long walk. Then we ate a big lunch.

2 get dressed in some strange clothes/join the festival/dance in the streets

3 meet our friends in town/watch the dancing/go home for a meal

4 go shopping/make a special lunch/eat lunch/play some games

9 On a piece of paper, write a paragraph describing an unusual event that you attended. Use these questions and Exercise 7 to help you.

- What was the event?
- When was it?
- Where was it?
- What did you do? (use sequence words)

CLIL PROJECT, page 140

Review: Units 11 & 12

Grammar (40 points)

1 Complete the sentences with the comparative or the superlative form. (6 points)

0 Carlos's computer is *faster than* David's. (fast)

00 Beyoncé is *the most talented* singer in the world. (talented)

1 Mexico is _____ Canada. (hot)

2 This TV show is _____ a movie. (interesting)

3 I'm _____ person in my family. (tall)

4 This new phone is _____ my old phone. (heavy)

5 My passport photo is _____ your photo. (bad)

6 My computer is _____ of all my gadgets. (useful)

2 Circle the correct answer. (4 points)

A: I need some new shoes.

B: What about these black ⁰ one / ~~ones~~?

A: They're boring. I like the brown ¹ one / ones.

B: OK. Which T-shirt are you going to buy? The white ² one / ones or the blue ³ one / ones?

A: I'm not sure. Excuse me, how much are these T-shirts?

C: They're $24.99 each.

A: Oh! Do you have any cheaper ⁴ one / ones?

3 Write the correct form of *be going to* and the verb in parentheses. (16 points)

Polly: What ⁰ *are you going to do* (do) in Italy this summer, Laura?

Laura: I ¹ _____ (learn) some Italian, I hope!

Polly: ² _____ (study) all summer?

Laura: No. We ³ _____ (spend) a week in Rome, too.

Polly: ⁴ _____ (David/go) with you?

Laura: No, ⁵ _____. He ⁶ _____ (stay) in Seattle.

Polly: What ⁷ _____ (he/do)?

Laura: He ⁸ _____ (not/do) anything!

4 Complete the sentences with *mine, yours, his, hers, ours,* or *theirs*. (5 points)

0 Is this his hat? No, it isn't. That's *his* over there. (he)

1 Whose books are these? They're _____. (we)

2 That isn't my phone. _____ is in my bag. (I)

3 Our house is big, but _____ is bigger. (they)

4 My pen is broken. Can I use _____? (you)

5 A: Whose jacket is this? B: It's _____. (she)

5 Unscramble the words in bold to make sentences with *want*. (4 points)

A: ⁰ you play Do to football want? *Do you want to play football?*

B: I'd like to, but ¹ **wants room Mom to me my clean.**

_____

A: But ² **we you us join to want!** You're really good! Maybe later?

_____

B: Thanks! But I can't this afternoon. My ³ **to car wants dad his me wash.**

_____

A: OK. ⁴ **want Do you to ask me David** to come to the movies with us on Saturday?

_____

B: Yes, great idea. I like David!

6 Complete the sentences. Use the adverb forms of the adjectives in the box. (5 points)

┌─────────────────────────────────────┐
│ • good • ~~loud~~ • angry • careful │
│ • hard • quick   │
└─────────────────────────────────────┘

0 Please speak *loudly*. I can't hear you.

1 Five minutes more! Please work _____ !

2 Jason works very _____ at school and always gets good grades.

3 Sally shouted _____ at her brother.

4 I'm sorry. I can't speak Spanish very _____ .

5 I always read the text _____ before I answer the questions.

Vocabulary (40 points)

7 Write the opposites of the adjectives.
(10 points)

0 heavy _light_

1 hard _____   6 slow _____
2 long _____   7 interesting _____
3 tall _____   8 big _____
4 dirty _____   9 new _____
5 far _____   10 expensive _____

8 Put the words in the correct group.
(19 points)

> • ~~baseball cap~~ • belt • boots • cardigan
> • coat • dress • hat • jacket • jeans • pants
> • sandals • shirt • shoes • shorts • skirt
> • sneakers • socks • sweater • top • T-shirt

Head	Body	Feet
baseball cap		

9 Complete the sentences with types of music.
(11 points)

a) I love ^{0} _classical_ music, especially Mozart.
b) What type of music do you prefer?
  ^{1} P __ p or ^{2} r __ p ?
c) My dad loves ^{3} j _____, but I prefer ^{4} r _____ k.
d) The best music for dancing is ^{5} s _____ and
  ^{6} r _____ n.
e) My brother hates ^{7} h _____ m _____
  music.
f) There are a lot of great American ^{8} s _____
  singers.
g) I love Bob Marley! Excuse me. Where are the
  ^{9} r _____ CDs?
h) This is a Taylor Swift song. Do you like
  ^{10} c _____ music?
l) My mother doesn't like my choice of music.
  She prefers ^{11} f _____ .

Use your English (20 points)

10 Circle the correct answer. (8 points)

0 **A:** Can I help you?
  B: a) Yes, I look for jeans. b) Yes, jeans please.
    c) Yes, I'm looking for some jeans.
1 **A:** Can I try these jeans on?
  B: a) They're a size 40. b) Yes, of course.
    c) Here you go.
2 **A:** Do you have any white T-shirts?
  B: a) Yes, there are some white ones here.
    b) No, sorry. I'll leave it. c) I'll take them.
3 **A:** Do they fit?
  B: a) They're a size 10. b) Yes, they're perfect.
    c) Yes, of course.
4 **A:** Do you have a smaller size?
  B: a) They're too small. b) They are smaller.
    c) Yes, here's a size 2.

11 Complete the conversation with the phrases
in the box. (12 points)

> • I'm sorry, I can't • At 8. • I'd love to.
> • ~~Would you like to~~ • does it start?
> • That would be great. • See you on Friday!

A: 0 ____ _Would you like to_ ____ watch the Olympics
at my house?
B: Yes, ^{1} _____ Is it on tonight?
A: No, it starts tomorrow night.
B: Oh, man. ^{2} _____ tomorrow.
I'm busy.
A: What about Friday?
B: OK. ^{3} _____ What time
  ^{4} _____
A: ^{5} _____
B: OK! ^{6} _____

SELF-CHECK	
Grammar	____ /40
Vocabulary	____ /40
Use your English	____ /20
Total score	____ /100

Extra practice

Unit 1

Lesson 1A, Vocabulary: Numbers

1 Write the missing number.

1 one three five seven _____*nine*_____

2 two four six _____ ten

3 five ten fifteen twenty _____

4 twenty nineteen eighteen _____ sixteen

5 fifty _____ seventy eighty ninety

Grammar

2 Number the conversation in the correct order.

☐ Thanks. And this is my sister Jessica.

☐ Hello, Jessica. How are you?

1 Hi. I'm Justin. What's your name?

☐ Not bad, thanks.

☐ My name's Ashlee.

☐ OK, thanks. And you?

☐ Ashlee! That's a cool name.

Lesson 1B

 Solve it!

1 What are the messages?

1 See you!

1 CU
2 GR82CU
3 RUOK?
4 CUL8R

Grammar

2 Register Miranda Cosgrove at the youth club. Complete the questions.

A: ¹ _____
_____?

B: Fine, thanks.

A: ² _____?

B: Miranda Taylor Cosgrove.

A: Miranda. That's a cool name.³ _____?

B: M-I-R-A-N-D-A.

A: ⁴ _____ last name?

B: C-O-S-G-R-O-V-E.

A: ⁵ _____?

B: 554 Hollywood Avenue, Los Angeles, California.

A: ⁶ _____?

B: (310) 890-9751.

A: Thank you, Miranda!

Lesson 1C, Vocabulary: Countries

1 Answer the questions in the quiz and complete the crossword puzzle.

World Quiz

Across

1 Where is spaghetti from?

3 What nationality is Keira Knightly?

6 What nationality is James Cameron?

Down

2 Where are kangaroos from?

4 Where is Tokyo?

5 Where are pandas from?

Grammar

2 Read about Paul and his band and complete the text with words from the box.

> • are • aren't • is • my (x2) • 're (x2) • they

My name ¹_____ Paul. This is ²_____ band, XPress. We ³_____ all at the same school but we ⁴_____ in the same grade. I'm in 9ᵗʰ grade. Jon and Mark ⁵_____ 15 and ⁶_____'re in 10ᵗʰ grade. We practice on Saturday morning in ⁷_____ garage. We aren't great but we ⁸_____ loud!

💡 Solve it!

3 Read Exercise 2 again. How old is Paul?

Unit 2

Lesson 2A, Grammar

1 Change sentences 2–4 to singular and sentences 6–8 to plural.

1 These are my notebooks.
  This is my notebook.

2 Where are my cell phones?
  _____

3 Those are ID cards.
  _____

4 Are your keys in my bag?
  _____

5 Is that your pen?
  Are those your pens?

6 This is a good sandwich.
  _____

7 Is this your book?
  _____

8 That's an apple.
  _____

Vocabulary: Common objects

2 Look at the pictures and complete the puzzle. Find the hidden word.

Lesson 2B, Grammar

1a Rewrite the questions in your notebook with the possessive *'s* or possessive *s'*.

1 What's your sisters name?
  What's your sister's name?
2 Who is your English teachers favorite actor?
3 In your class, what is the boys favorite band?
4 In your class, who is the girls favorite singer?
5 What is your English teachers favorite city?
6 In your class, what is the students favorite sport?

b GROUPS Find out the answers to the questions above for your group.

2 Danny is at a party at Carla's house. Complete the conversation with *my, your, his, her, our,* or *their.*

Danny: Who's that, Carla?

Carla: That's ¹ _____my_____ sister. ² _____ name's Emily. Those two people are ³ _____ parents.

Danny: And who are they?

Carla: They're my cousins. ⁴ _____ names are Tim and Sarah. Tim, come and meet ⁵ _____ friend, Danny.

Danny: Hi, Tim. Are you and Sarah from Seattle?

Tim: No, ⁶ _____ hometown is Phoenix.

Danny: Cool! I love Phoenix. Listen. This is my favorite singer, Adam Lambert. ⁷ _____ new CD is really good. Who's ⁸ _____ favorite singer?

Tim: I don't have a favorite singer. But I like The Black Eyed Peas. I have ⁹ _____ new album here.

Danny: Great. Let's listen.

Lesson 2C, Vocabulary: Fast food

1 Complete the words (1–6) and write the missing price (7).

Jamie's Café
BILL

¹ W _ _ _ _ r	$1.00
² _ _ ips	$ .75
³ C _ _ _ ee	$ .50
⁴ _ ea	$1.20
⁵ _ _ _ ger	$4.50
⁶ _ _ _ cream	⁷ $ _ _
Total	**$10.45**

2 Complete the conversation.

A: ¹ _____ sandwich, please?

B: Chicken or cheese?

A: ² _____ , please.

B: OK, one chicken sandwich.

A: ³ _____ orange juice, please?

B: OK. One orange juice and one chicken sandwich. Anything else?

A: No, that's it. ⁴ _____ altogether?

B: It's $6.50.

A: ⁵ _____ go.

B: Thanks.

Unit 3
Lesson 3A, Grammar

Complete the conversation with *there is, there's, there isn't, there's no,* or *Is there.*

Mom: How's your apartment?

Sandra: It's OK. ¹ ___There's___ a bedroom and a living room.

Mom: ² _____ a bathroom?

Sandra: Yes, ³ _____ but ⁴ _____ a bathtub, only a shower.

Mom: ⁵ _____ a washing machine?

Sandra: Yes, ⁶ _____ but the kitchen is awful. The stove's OK but ⁷ _____ dishwasher.

Dad: No dishwasher? So what's the problem? ⁸ _____ a sink and hot water!

Lesson 3B, Vocabulary: Furniture

1 Find nine items of furniture in the wordsearch.

W	A	R	D	R	O	B	E	B
T	A	B	E	D	T	V	B	L
A	R	S	H	E	L	F	K	K
B	M	L	L	N	A	B	M	S
L	C	N	G	M	M	P	I	O
E	H	M	R	Y	P	N	R	F
C	A	B	I	N	E	T	R	A
R	I	N	D	M	G	R	O	G
K	R	D	E	S	K	D	R	T

Grammar

2 Complete the conversation with the correct form of *there is/are*. Use *some* or *any* if possible.

Melissa: ¹ _____There's_____ a new coffee shop on Fuller Street. It's really nice.

Andrew: Is it an Internet café?

Melissa: Yes, it is. ² _____ six computers.

Andrew: Great! ³ _____ sofas or armchairs?

Melissa: Yes, ⁴ _____.

⁵ _____ two big sofas and ⁶ _____ nice armchairs.

Andrew: ⁷ _____ a television?

Melissa: Yes, ⁸ _____, but ⁹ _____ a DVD player. And one more thing, ¹⁰ _____ a really nice waitress on Saturdays.

Andrew: Who's that?

Melissa: Me!

Lesson 3C, Grammar, Vocabulary: Furniture

1 Look at Picture A and name the numbered items in your notebook.

2 Look at the two pictures and find six differences.

Picture A	Picture B
The magazines are on the shelf.	The magazines are under the bed.

Unit 4

Lesson 4A, Grammar

1 In your notebook, write affirmative, negative, or interrogative sentences with the correct form of *have*.

1 I/small family ✓ *I have a small family.*
2 I/any sisters ✗ *I don't have any sisters.*
3 My grandparents/a big house ✗
4 you/any brothers?
5 My brother and I/ten cousins ✓
6 We/a big yard ✗
7 you/a TV in your bedroom?
8 They/any grandparents ✗

Vocabulary: Family

 Solve it!

2 In your notebook, draw a family tree for Donna and James.

Donna is 16 and James is 13. Their parents are Louis and Julia. Julia's sister is Lucy and her husband's name is Roger. Their children are Greg and Ann. Julia and Lucy's parents are John and Mary.

Lesson 4B, Vocabulary: Physical descriptions

 Solve it!

Look at the photos and complete the information about the famous people with words of appearance. Can you name the people?

Hair: _____, _____
Eyes: _____
Other adjectives: _____

Hair: _____, _____
Eyes: _____
Other adjectives: _____

Lesson 4C, Vocabulary: Months and seasons

1 Complete the crossword with the correct months.

Across

2 The third month of the year.

5 This month has two syllables and the third letter is *L*.

7 A month beginning with *F*.

8 The month after August.

Down

1 This month has the letter *O* in it.

2 This month has three letters.

3 The sixth month of the year.

4 The month after March.

6 The eighth month of the year.

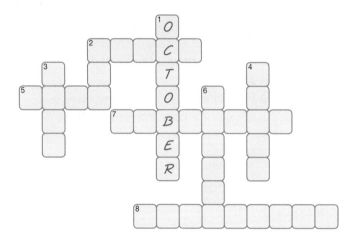

2 In your notebook, write sentences about the events and say when they are.

Event	Season	Day	Date
1 The Cup Final	spring	Saturday	5/4
2 The Boat Show	winter	Friday	1/5
3 The School Open House	spring	Wednesday	3/31
4 The Youth Games	summer	Sunday	7/12
5 The Fruit Fair	fall	Tuesday	10/21
6 The Music Festival	summer	Saturday and Sunday	8/2 and 8/3

1 The Cup Final is in the spring. This year it's on Saturday, May 4.

Unit 5

Lesson 5A, Vocabulary: Occupations

1 Look at the pictures and complete the puzzle with the occupations.

Down   **Across**

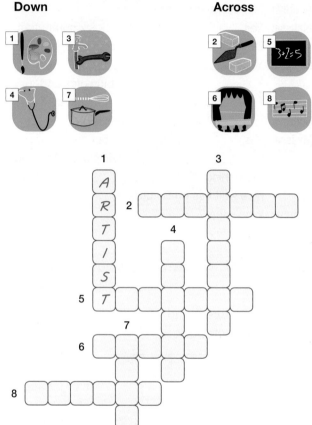

Grammar

2 Complete the text about Maya Suarez with the verbs in the box.

• have • live • 'm from • speak • work

www.dreamjobs.com

DREAM JOBS

My name is Maya Suarez. I'm 25 years old and I [1] *'m from* Costa Rica. I'm an artist. I [2] _____ for Pearson Education in the U.S. I draw illustrations for books. I [3] _____ Spanish, English, and French. I [4] _____ with my friends in New York. We [5] _____ an apartment in Manhattan. Life is good!

Lesson 5B, Vocabulary: Places of work

 Solve it!

1 Read the clues and complete the chart.

1 Joe is a secretary.

2 Jack is from Miami in the U.S.

Name	Country	Job	Place of work
Joe		*secretary*	
Jack	*U.S.*		
Jim			

3 Jim works on a construction site.

4 The American works in a hospital.

5 The plumber is from Montreal, Canada.

6 The person from London works in an office.

7 The person who works at the hospital is a nurse.

2 Helen Santos is a secretary. Complete phrases 1–3. Then match them with phrases a–c and write a paragraph in your notebook.

Helen Santos is a secretary. She works in ...

1 She/work/in an office	a) which takes a half hour.
2 She/live/in Scarsdale,	b) 8 to 12 hours a day.
3 She/take/the train,	c) a town in New York.

Lesson 5C, Grammar

Complete the conversation with an object pronoun.

> • her • him • it (x 2) • me • ~~them~~ • us

Laura: Where are the pizzas?

Polly: I have [1] _____ *them* _____ here. Look, that new show, *High Life,* is on TV. What do you think of [2] _____ ?

Laura: I think Brad's girlfriend is awful. I hate [3] _____ !

Polly: Me, too. What about Brad?

Laura: Oh, I love [4] _____ . He's cool!

Laura: Eww! This pizza's terrible! I don't like [5] _____ .

Polly: Great! You can give it to [6] _____ !

David: Hey! Carlos and I are hungry, too. Can you leave [7] _____ some pizza?

Laura: Too late! Sorry.

Unit 6

Lesson 6A, Vocabulary: Clock times

Look at the online movie schedule. Write questions and answers for each movie.

A: *What time does Transformers 3 start?*

B: *It starts at six forty-five and again at nine twenty.*

Click on a movie to buy your tickets		
Movie	**Times**	
1 Transformers 3	6:45	9:20
2 Harry Potter	3:10	5:35
3 Zookeeper	1:30	4:05
4 Captain America	7:35	10:15

Lesson 6B, Vocabulary: Daily routines

 Solve it!

1 Match the verbs in column A with the words in column B.

A		B	
1	go to _*b*_	a)	music
2	watch _____	b)	school
3	take _____	c)	your friends
4	play _____	d)	homework
5	listen to _____	e)	a book
6	do _____	f)	television
7	brush _____	g)	a shower
8	have _____	h)	video games
9	call _____	i)	your teeth
10	read _____	j)	breakfast

Lesson 6C, Grammar

Complete the conversation with the correct word.

Carlos: How [1] _____ *often* _____ do you exercise?

Polly: [2] _____ day.

Carlos: [3] _____ ! [4] _____ great.

Polly: How often [5] _____ you exercise?

Carlos: About four [6] _____ a month.

Polly: Hmm. That's not [7] _____ .

Carlos: I know. I'm very lazy!

Unit 7

Lesson 7A, Vocabulary: Verbs of ability

1 In your notebook, write sentences for the pictures using *can* or *can't*.

1 She can't ride a horse.

Grammar

2 Complete the conversation using the correct form of *can*.

A: There's a talent show next Saturday at the youth club. What ¹_____ you do?

B: A talent show! Oh, no! I ²_____ sing or dance!

A: That's OK. Maybe you ³_____ do something else. ⁴_____ you juggle?

B: No, I ⁵_____, but I ⁶_____ act. What about you?

A: Well, my sisters ⁷_____ sing, and I ⁸_____ play the guitar. Our favorite song is *Bluebird*.

B: That's great! See you at the show!

Lesson 7B, Vocabulary: Food

1 Find ten more food words in the wordsearch. The count nouns are in the plural form.

E	F	B	Y	S	U	G	A	R	O
C	S	R	K	H	B	P	V	I	C
C	U	E	O	N	I	O	N	S	A
H	P	A	X	B	U	T	T	E	R
E	W	D	G	A	D	A	D	B	R
E	M	E	V	N	G	T	J	I	O
S	T	O	M	A	T	O	E	S	T
E	L	Z	B	N	Q	E	Y	R	S
O	T	Y	D	A	J	S	D	V	N
A	E	G	G	S	T	M	I	L	K

Grammar

2 Complete the telephone conversation with the cues and *some* or *any*.

Mom: Hi, Olivia.

Olivia: Hi, Mom. Where are you?

Mom: I'm at the supermarket. Can you look in the kitchen cabinets? ¹ *Do we have any eggs?* (do we have/eggs/?)

Olivia: No, we don't. And we ²_____. (don't have/ potatoes/✗).

Mom: OK. ³_____ (there/butter or milk) in the refrigerator?

Olivia: ⁴_____, (there/butter/✓) but ⁵_____ (there/ milk/✗).

Mom: OK. One more thing. ⁶_____? (do we have/ tomatoes)

Olivia: No, we don't. ⁷_____ (there/carrots and onions/✓), but ⁸_____. (there/ tomatoes/✗)

Mom: OK, see you soon.

Olivia: Bye, Mom.

Lesson 7C, Grammar

1 Complete the sentences with the affirmative or negative imperative of the verbs in the box.

> • ask (x 2)   • go   • leave   • open   • send
> • show   • wait

1 Here's your birthday present.
___*Don't open*___ it before Monday!

2 A: I have a message from Sam.
  B: _____ me.

3 _____ in the store. I'm coming.

4 _____ your bag on the floor. It
isn't safe.

5 _____ Sam. He doesn't know.
_____ me!

6 _____ me a postcard from
New York!

7 Please _____ yet. It's still early.

2 Look at the map and complete these directions.

Hi Jed!
Come to my house at about six o'clock tonight
to watch a DVD. My address is 71 Walton Street.
There's an Indian ¹ _____
² _____ the house and a big
³ _____ behind it. Don't worry!
My house is ⁴ _____ the train
station. Here's a map to help you.
See you!
Joe
P.S. There's an Internet café ⁵ _____
the restaurant, so wait there if I'm not at home!

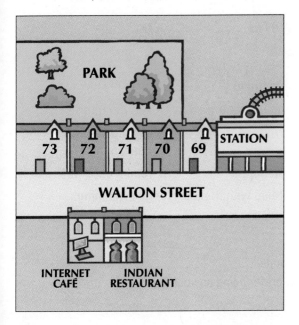

Unit 8

Lesson 8A, Vocabulary: Weather

 Solve it!

1 Look at the clues and complete the weather
word puzzle. What is hidden word number 8?

Clues

4 Not cold but
   not very hot.

1 It's . . .

5 It's . . .

2 It's . . .   6 Very cold.

3 It's . . .   7 It's . . .

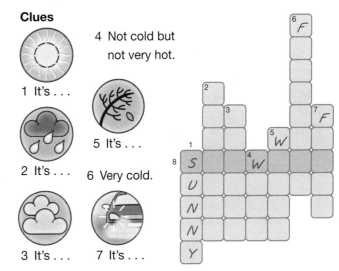

Grammar

2 Look at the pictures and write questions and
answers in your notebook.

1 you/watch iCarly? ✗ watch/movie
  A: *Are you watching iCarly?*
  B: *No, I'm not. I'm watching a movie.*

2 he/do his homework? ✗ write/an email

3 they/watch television? ✗ play/a video game

4 she/sit on the floor? ✗ lie/on the sofa

5 you/take a shower? ✗/take a bath

6 it/rain? ✗/snow

Lesson 8B, Grammar

1 In your notebook, write sentences using the simple present or present continuous.

1 David's mom/usually/work/five days a week.

2 She/not work/today, because she's on vacation.

3 She/not usually/cook breakfast, but today she/cook/breakfast for David.

4 David often/have/cereal for breakfast, but today he/have/eggs.

5 Today he/walk/to school, but he usually/take/a bus.

2 Complete the soccer commentary with the correct form of the simple present or present continuous.

"Hello, and welcome to *Sports Live*! It's a sunny day here in Lisbon, and the Portuguese team ¹_____ (come) onto the soccer field now. And there's Ronaldo. Cristiano Ronaldo usually ²_____ (play) soccer for Real Madrid in Spain, but today, he ³_____ (play) an international match for his home country, Portugal. He ⁴_____ (run) and he ⁵_____ (wave) at the crowd. He ⁶_____ (live) in Madrid now, but he usually ⁷_____ (come) back to Portugal on vacation. What a great player!"

Lesson 8C, Vocabulary: Free-time activities

1a PAIRS Do the quiz with your partner and note your partner's answers in your notebook.

A: *Do you prefer going shopping with a friend or going to the movies?*
B: *I prefer going shopping with a friend.*

b GROUPS Tell the group about your partner.

Joanna prefers going shopping with a friend.

Free-time personality quiz

What kind of person are you? Do the quiz and find out.

	Do you prefer . . . **A**	Or . . . **B**
1 It's Saturday afternoon.	• go shop with a friend	• go to the movies
2 It's your turn on the computer.	• chat with friends online	• surf the Internet
3 You're at home after school.	• play video games with a friend	• listen to music in your room
4 It's Sunday.	• hang out with friends	• read a good book
5 It's a sunny afternoon.	• go skateboarding with friends	• go swimming

CHECK YOUR SCORE!

Mostly As: You are very sociable. You like doing things with friends.

Mostly Bs: You are a friendly but quiet person. Sometimes you prefer being on your own.

Unit 9

Lesson 9A, Grammar

1 Write full questions and answers.

1 A: How/your vacation last month?

2 B: Really good.

　A: *How was your vacation last month?*

　B: *It was really good.*

3 A: What/weather like?　4 B: Warm and sunny

5 A: Hotel/nice?　6 B: Yes but/next to a train station

7 A: People/friendly?　8 B: Yes/very nice

9 A: Food/good?　10 B: No but/cheap!

2 Find the mistakes below and correct the information. Write the sentences in your notebook.

1 The Beatles were movie stars.

　The Beatles weren't movie stars. They were

　pop stars.

2 Abraham Lincoln was British.

3 Picasso was a Mexican artist.

4 Pelé and Maradona were famous basketball players.

5 Henry VIII was a French king.

6 Pavarotti was an Argentinian singer.

Now check your answers at the bottom of the page.

Lesson 9B, Grammar

1 Rewrite the diary entries with the simple past of the verbs in parentheses.

Sunday

We ^1_____ (arrive) here in Chicago at ten o'clock at night. I ^2_____ (try) to call John, but he ^3_____ (not answer) his phone. Maybe he ^4_____ (be) asleep. I ^5_____ (decide) to send him an email.

Monday

We ^6_____ (walk) to Lincoln Square, but it ^7_____ (start) to rain so we ^8_____ (not stay) long. The rain ^9_____ (not stop) for three hours! In the afternoon, we ^10_____ (walk) along Lincoln Avenue and ^11_____ (look) at the shops. I ^12_____ (not want) to buy anything. Everything ^13_____ (be) very expensive. We ^14_____ (want) to go to the Sears Tower, but it ^15_____ (close) at 8 P.M.

 Solve it!

2 Jake, Susie, Gina, and Mark were in a race. Read the clues. What was their position (1st, 2nd, 3rd, or 4th) and what color were their T-shirts (red, blue, green, or yellow)?

Name	Position	Color of T-shirt
Jake		
Susie		
Gina		
Mark		

1 Jake finished after Mark.

2 Jake didn't wear a green T-shirt.

3 Susie finished in front of Mark.

4 Gina's T-shirt was yellow.

5 Gina started slowly but finished first.

6 Susie wasn't in a red T-shirt.

7 Mark decided to wear a blue T-shirt.

Lesson 9C, Vocabulary: Adjectives of feeling

Solve it!

1 Complete the crossword puzzle with an adjective of feeling. Find the hidden word.

1 You are watching a three-hour movie about the history of the refrigerator.
2 You played sports yesterday and you stayed up late last night.
3 Your brother takes your cell phone from your bedroom. He doesn't ask.
4 There is a concert tomorrow. You and your friends have tickets for it.
5 Your friends are at a concert, but you can't go. You don't have any money.

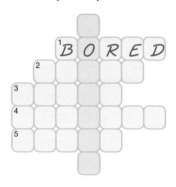

Grammar

2 Look at Luke's "To Do" list for yesterday and write conversations in your notebook. Use the example as a model.

Luke's "To Do" list

1 watch a movie (✓ The Green Lantern)
2 chat with a friend online (✓ Juan)
3 play a sport (✓ volleyball)
4 study for an exam (✓ English exam)
5 cook dinner for Linda (✓ pasta)

You: *Did you watch a movie yesterday?*
Luke: *Yes, I did.*
You: *What movie did you watch?*
Luke: *I watched The Green Lantern.*

Unit 10

Lesson 10A, Vocabulary: Transportation

1 What forms of transportation can you see in the photos? What forms of transportation are not in the photos? Complete the chart.

In photo 1	In photo 2	Not in photos 1 or 2
car	*train*	

Grammar

2 Complete the story with a verb from the box in the simple past.

• do • drive • ~~go~~ • not find • not take • say • take

Two soccer fans from Barcelona ¹_____*went*_____ to Berlin last week for a Spain–Germany game. Elias and Manuel ²_____ a plane because Elias hates flying. They ³_____. In Berlin they parked the car, and Manuel ⁴_____ a photo of the street name. They watched the game and ⁵_____ some shopping. Then they looked for the car for 40 minutes. They ⁶_____ it so they showed the photo of the street name to a police officer.

"That's not a street name" the policeman ⁷_____ in English. "It means 'Don't park here' in German!"

Lesson 10B, Grammar

1 In your notebook, complete the questions in Jenny's e-mail to her friend Gustavo.

1 Where did you go?

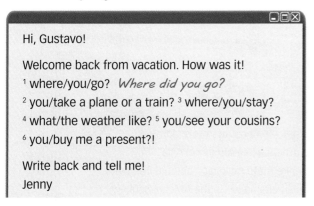

Hi, Gustavo!

Welcome back from vacation. How was it!
¹ where/you/go? *Where did you go?*
² you/take a plane or a train? ³ where/you/stay?
⁴ what/the weather like? ⁵ you/see your cousins?
⁶ you/buy me a present?!

Write back and tell me!
Jenny

2 In your notebook, write Gustavo's answers.

Hi Jenny,
My vacation was awesome . . .

Lesson 10C, Vocabulary: Landforms

1 Look at the pictures and complete the crossword puzzle. What's the hidden place (number 9)?

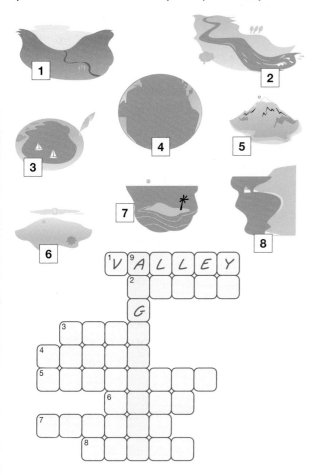

Grammar

2 Use the information in the chart to write sentences using *ago* in your notebook.

1 John went to the train station 45 minutes ago.

When?	Now
1 John/go/train station/ 2:30.	3:15
2 They/see/the Eiffel Tower/Monday.	Wednesday
3 My sister/visit/ Germany/2005.	2010
4 I/climb/the mountain/ Tuesday, July 3.	Tuesday, July 10

Unit 11

Lesson 11A, Vocabulary: Short adjectives

1 Complete the crossword puzzle with the opposite of the adjectives.

Across: 1 long 5 new 7 heavy 9 cold
10 expensive 12 hard 13 old 14 good

Down: 1 fast 2 short (person) 3 short (river)
4 slow 6 clean 8 light 10 dirty 11 hot

Grammar

2a Complete the questions with the correct comparative or superlative form of the adjective in parentheses.

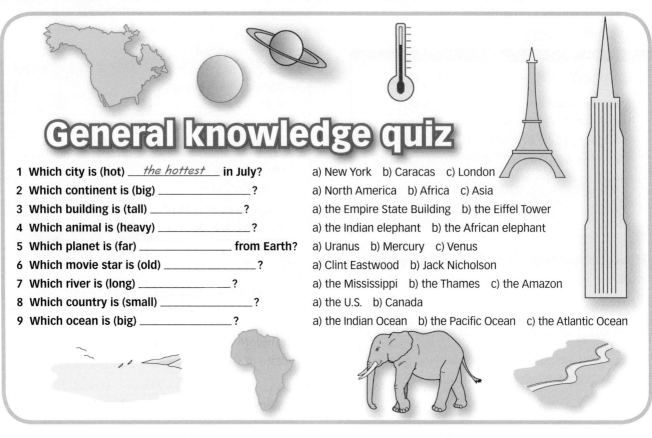

General knowledge quiz

1 Which city is (hot) ___the hottest___ in July?
2 Which continent is (big) _____?
3 Which building is (tall) _____?
4 Which animal is (heavy) _____?
5 Which planet is (far) _____ from Earth?
6 Which movie star is (old) _____?
7 Which river is (long) _____?
8 Which country is (small) _____?
9 Which ocean is (big) _____?

a) New York   b) Caracas   c) London
a) North America   b) Africa   c) Asia
a) the Empire State Building   b) the Eiffel Tower
a) the Indian elephant   b) the African elephant
a) Uranus   b) Mercury   c) Venus
a) Clint Eastwood   b) Jack Nicholson
a) the Mississippi   b) the Thames   c) the Amazon
a) the U.S.   b) Canada
a) the Indian Ocean   b) the Pacific Ocean   c) the Atlantic Ocean

b Now test yourself! Answer the questions.

Lesson 11B, Vocabulary: Adjectives of quality

Complete the sentences with *a* or *an* and an adjective from the box.

| • attractive • ~~beautiful~~ • boring • dangerous • exciting • famous • talented • useful |

1 Rome is ___a beautiful___ city. You must see it.
2 Golf is _____ sport. I don't like it at all.
3 Zac Efron is _____ actor. He always looks good.
4 Roger Federer is _____ tennis player. He's better than the others.
5 Beyoncé is _____ singer. Everyone knows Beyoncé.
6 Autoracing is _____ sport. There are always accidents.
7 *Harry Potter and the Order of the Phoenix* is _____ book. I read it in one day.
8 My digital camera is not _____ gadget. I never use it.

Lesson 11C, Grammar

1a Number the conversation in the correct order. Then complete it with *one* or *ones*.

☐ That's expensive. Do you have any cheaper
a) _____?

☐ OK. Here's a medium. Does it fit?

☐ Yes! I'll take it.

☐ The brown b) _____? It's $29.99.

☑ Excuse me, how much is that hoodie in the window?

☐ Try c) _____ on? Of course. What size are you?

☐ Cheaper? Yes, we do. These blue
d) _____ over here are only $19.99.

☐ Great. Can I try e) _____ on?

☐ I'm a medium.

b Now write a similar conversation about some sneakers.

Unit 12

Lesson 12A, Vocabulary: Types of music

1 Find eight types of music in the wordsearch.

W	R	A	T	E	C	H	N	O
C	O	R	Z	Z	D	L	N	S
J	C	X	P	H	L	O	S	O
A	K	G	O	F	O	L	K	U
Z	R	U	P	J	A	B	Y	L
Z	O	R	E	A	L	D	K	M
C	L	A	S	S	I	C	A	L
X	A	P	L	L	W	J	E	P

Grammar

2 Complete the conversation using *going to* and one of the verbs in the box.

> • get • ~~go~~ • stay (x3) • take (x2)

Tom: Where are you ¹ _going to go_ on vacation?

Hannah: To San Francisco.

Tom: Are you ² _____ a plane?

Hannah: No, I hate planes.

Tom: So how are you ³ _____ there?

Hannah: I'm ⁴ _____ a train.

Tom: Are you ⁵ _____ in a hotel?

Hannah: No, I'm not. Hotels are too expensive.

Tom: So where are you ⁶ _____?

Hannah: At a youth hostel.

Tom: And how long are you ⁷ _____?

Hannah: For two weeks.

Tom: Cool!

Lesson 12B, Grammar

1 Complete the conversation with a possessive pronoun or a name + possessive 's.

Liz: Is this your CD?

Frank: No, it isn't ¹ _____ mine _____. It's ² (Sarah) _____ .

Liz: And what about this heavy-metal CD? Is it ³ (you) _____ ?

Frank: No, I think it's ⁴ (Henry) _____ .

Liz: No, it isn't. Maybe Martin and Claudia left it.

Frank: You're right. It's ⁵ (they) _____ .

Liz: And Martin left his jacket, too. Look, this is ⁶ (he) _____ .

Frank: Yes, and this is Claudia's R&B CD.

Liz: No, it isn't ⁷ (she) _____ . It's ⁸ (we) _____ . We bought it yesterday, remember?

Vocabulary: Adverbs

2 Change the adjectives in the box to adverbs and complete the sentences.

> • careless • good • hard • late • ~~loud~~ • slow

1 My brother usually plays his music very _loudly_ .

2 When I'm tired, I walk to school _____ .

3 On Saturdays I get up _____ .

4 Our teachers work really _____ .

5 Our team is great. They usually play _____ .

6 My sister gets bad grades when she does her homework _____ .

Lesson 12C, Grammar

1 Rearrange the words to make sentences. Write them in your notebook.

1 wants our She to rooms. us clean
  She wants us to clean our rooms.

2 Russian. I to want learn don't

3 you Do to want you? me help

4 do I again. you to this want exercise

5 want Does movie? see she that to

6 her He go the wants to concert. to

2 Write a conversation. Use your imagination!

James: Would you like to come to the Rihanna concert?

James   **Kim**

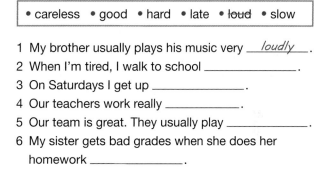

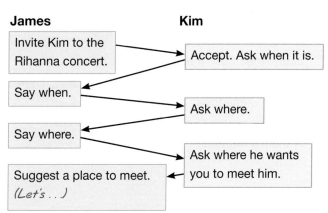

Pronunciation

Unit 1

Lesson 1A Exercise 11
(1 6)

/ɪ/ fifty

Listen and write the numbers.

a) _50_   b) _____   c) _____   d) _____   e) _____

Lesson 1C Exercise 5
(1 15)

Word stress

Listen and repeat. Then mark the stress.

a) Argentina b) Australia c) Brazil d) Canada
e) Chile f) China g) France h) Greece i) Italy
j) Japan k) Madagascar l) Mexico m) Poland
n) Portugal o) Russia p) Spain q) Sudan
r) Turkey s) the U.K. t) the U.S.

Unit 2

Lesson 2A Exercise 5

/ə/ camera

a (1 20) Listen and repeat.

camera banana common Portugal

b (1 21) Listen and underline the /ə/ sounds. Then say the sentences.

1 A: Is that a new camera?
   B: Yes, it's from Portugal.
2 Can I have two bananas?

Unit 3

Lesson 3A Exercise 8

/ð/ there

a (1 34) Listen and repeat.

there the this that

b (1 35) Listen and underline the /ð/ sounds. Then say the sentences.

There's a big kitchen. Is that the bathroom?
Is there a bathtub?

Unit 4

Lesson 4C Exercise 6

/θ/ three

a (1 52) Listen and repeat.

three third fourth think thirty month fifth birthday

b (1 53) Listen and complete the sentences.

1 Three _____ and _____ days.
2 Jonathan's _____ birthday is on May _____ .

Unit 5

Lesson 5B Exercise 4

/ʌ/ does

a (2 7) Listen and repeat. Then underline the stress.

does doesn't from

b (2 8) Listen and underline the /ʌ/ sound in the sentences.

1 My uncle is from Colombia.
2 My brother doesn't speak Russian.

Unit 6

Lesson 6C Exercise 6

/o/ open

a (2 22) Listen and repeat.

open close home go no

b (2 23) Listen and underline the /o/ sounds.

1 I want to know when the museum opens.
2 Oh, no! The store closes in five minutes.
3 I go home at 3 o'clock.

Unit 7

Lesson 7A Exercise 8

/æ/ c<u>a</u>n

a (2/29) Listen and repeat.

1 Yes, I can. 2 They're Italian. 3 My hat is black.

b (2/30) Listen and underline the /æ/ sounds in the sentences.

1 Can Sam swim? Yes, he can.
2 A: That's a cool hat.
   B: Thanks!
3 My dad thinks the movie is bad, but I think it's fantastic.

Unit 8

Lesson 8A Exercise 5

/ŋ/ doi<u>ng</u>

a (2/42) Listen and repeat.

doing making playing ringing singing

b (2/43) Underline the /ŋ/ sounds in the sentences, then listen and check.

Something is wrong. She's singing the wrong song.

Unit 9

Lesson 9A Exercise 5

/h/ <u>h</u>ow

a (3/3) Listen and repeat.

how he who his house

b (3/4) Listen and underline the /h/ sounds.

Hello. How are you? Who's he? How did you get home? How's Harry? Who's his friend?

Unit 10

Lesson 10A Exercise 8

/ɑ/ c<u>ar</u>

a (3/15) Listen and repeat.

car lot hot father bottle

b (3/16) Listen and underline the /ɑ/ sounds. Then repeat the conversation in pairs.

A: It's six o'clock. Let's start.
B: We can't. Oscar and Anya aren't here.
A: Why not? Is their car in the parking lot?
B: I don't know. I'll call them. Maybe they're looking for a parking spot.

Unit 11

Lesson 11C Exercise 6

/ʃ/ <u>sh</u>irt

a (3/29) Listen and repeat.

shirt shorts shoes shopping washing machine station

b (3/30) Listen and underline the /ʃ/ sounds in the conversation.

A: Hi, Sherry. Are you going shopping?
B: Yes, I am. I need a new pair of shorts and a T-shirt.

Unit 12

Lesson 12A Exercise 8

/ʤ/ <u>j</u>azz

a (3/35) Listen and repeat.

jazz jogging gymnastics biology college

b (3/36) Listen and underline the /ʤ/ sounds in the conversation.

A: Jerry, what job do you want to do after college?
B: I want to be a jazz musician.

Hello!

Complete the examples and the grammar rules that follow.

Lesson 1A, page 4 and Lesson 1C, page 9

The verb *be*: Statements

Affirmative	Negative
I'm 13.	I'm not 14.
You're 13.	You **aren't** 14. OR You're **not** 14.
He's 13.	He **isn't** 14. OR He__ _____ 14.
She__ 13.	She _____ 14. OR She__ _____ 14.
It__ new.	It _____ old. OR It __ _____ old.
We're 13.	We **aren't** 14. OR We're **not** 14.
They're 13.	They **aren't** 14. OR They're **not** 14.

Short forms (contractions)

I am = I'm	I'm not
You are = You're	You **aren't** / You're **not**
He is = He's	He **isn't** / He's **not**
She is = She's	She **isn't** / She's **not**
It is = It's	It **isn't** / It's **not**
We are = We're	We **aren't** / We're **not**
They are = They're	They **aren't** / They're **not**

- The present of *be* has three forms: *am,* _____, and *are*.
- The pronoun _____ is both singular and plural.
- The short form of *he is* is _____.
- The short form of *it is* is _____.
- The short form of *is not* is _____.
- The short form of *I am not* is _____.

Lesson 1A, page 4 and Lesson 1C, page 9

The verb *be*: Questions

Yes/No Questions	Short answers

Am I 13?	Yes, you **are**.
	    No, you **aren't**. OR
	    No, you're **not**.

Are you 13?	Yes, I **am**. No, I'm **not**.

_____ he/she/it 13?	Yes, he/she/it _____.
	    No, he/she/it **isn't**. OR
	    No, he/she/it__ _____.

Are we/they 13?	Yes, we/they **are**.
	    No, we **aren't**. OR
	    No, we're **not**.

Information questions	Short answers
What's his name?	Zach.
How old is he?	He's 20.
Where's he from?	He's from Cuba.
When's his birthday?	July 21.

Short forms (contractions)

What is = What's	**Where is** = Where's
When is = When's	

- In questions, the verb *be* comes before the _____.
- After *yes* and *no*, use a _____.

Lesson 1A, page 5 and Lesson 2B, page 15

Subject pronouns	Possessive adjectives
I	**My** book is new.
You	_____ book is new.
He	_____ book is new.
She	_____ book is new.
It	**Its** title is cool. (not *it's*)
They	**Their** books are new.
We	**Our** books are new.

- Possessive adjectives show possession. They come before _____.
- The possessive form of *it* is _____.

2 Your life

Complete the examples and the grammar rules that follow.

Lesson 2A, page 13

Indefinite articles: *a*, *an*

a pencil	**an** apple
_____ watch	_____ MP3 player
_____ diary	_____ ID card

- Use the article _____ before a singular noun that begins with a consonant sound.
- Use _____ before a singular noun that begins with a vowel sound.

Lesson 2A, page 13

Regular nouns: Plural

Singular	Plural
pencil	pencils
b<u>oy</u>	boys
diar<u>y</u>	diaries
watch	watches
class	classes
toma<u>to</u>	tomatoes
radi<u>o</u>	radios
lif<u>e</u>	lives

Irregular nouns: Plural

child = **children**   man = **men**   woman = **women**
Note: *People* is always plural.

- Most nouns form their plurals by adding -s or _____.
- Nouns that end in a consonant + -y, change -y to _____ and add _____.
- Nouns that end in a consonant + -o, add _____.
- The plural form of irregular nouns varies.

Lesson 2A, page 13

This, that, these, those

This is a pen.

_____ is an MP3 player.

_____ are notebooks.

Those are keys.

- When *this*, *these*, *that*, and *those* replace nouns, they are called demonstrative pronouns.
- Use _____ to talk about one thing that is near you.
- Use _____ to talk about things that are far from you.

Lesson 2B, page 15

Possessive (*'s*) (singular nouns)	Possessive (*s'*) (plural nouns)
David**'s** shoes	their parents**'** car
Tony___ brother	my student___ names
Irregular plural nouns	
The children**'s** toys	The men___ coats

- Add an apostrophe + s (*'s*) to a _____ noun to show possession.
- Add an apostrophe (*'*) to a _____ noun that ends in -s to show possession.
- Add ___ to an irregular plural noun to show possession.

Lesson 2C, page 17

How much is/How much are

Question	Answer
How much is a sandwich?	It's $5.50.
How much _____ a bottle of water?	A dollar.
How much _____ the juice?	It's $2.00.
How much are the sandwiches?	They're $5.50 each.
How much _____ chips?	They're 99¢ a bag.

- Use *How much* _____ to ask about the price of one item and of noncount nouns.
- Use *How much* _____ to ask about the prices of plural count nouns.

129

3 Homes

Complete the examples and the grammar rules that follow.

Lesson 3A, page 23 and Lesson 3B, page 25

There is/There isn't; There are/There aren't

Affirmative	Negative
There's a bathroom over there.	There's no bathroom here.
There's hot water in the kitchen.	There isn't any cold water.
There are two bathrooms over there.	There aren't any bathrooms here.

Question	Short answers
_____ there a bathroom here?	Yes, there is. No, there isn't.
_____ there any bathrooms here?	Yes, _____ _____. No, _____ _____.

- Use *There* _____ to say that something exists in a particular location.
- Use _____ *a* to say the location of things or the time of an event.
  ***There's** a concert on Friday at my school.*

Lesson 3A, page 23

Definite article: *the*

A: Where's your mom?
B: She's in **the** kitchen.
A: Is _____ kitchen this way?

- Use *the* when you and the person you're speaking with are talking about the same thing. (**Note:** In the example, speakers *A* and *B* are talking about the same kitchen.)
- Use *the* for a person, place, or thing that is unique—there's only one.
  ***The** moon is beautiful!*
  Does _____ earth revolve around _____ sun?

Lesson 3B, page 25

Some and *any*

Affirmative	Negative
There are some chairs over there.	There _____ any chairs here.
Questions	**Short answers**
Are _____ any pens in this box?	Yes, there _____. No, _____ aren't.

- In statements beginning with *There are*, use *some* + _____ nouns.
- In statements beginning with *There aren't*, use _____ + plural nouns.
- Use *Are there* + _____ in *yes/no* questions.

Lesson 3C, page 27

Prepositions of place

The ball is **in** the box.

The ball is _____ the box.

The ball is _____ the box.

The ball is _____ the box.

The ball is _____ the box.

The ball is _____ the box.

- A preposition + a noun is called a prepositional phrase.

4 Families

Complete the examples and the grammar rules that follow.

Lesson 4A, page 31 and Lesson 4B, page 33

Have/Has

Affirmative	Negative
I **have** a sister.	I **don't have** any brothers.
You _____ a sister.	You **don't have** any brothers.
He **has** a brother.	He **doesn't have** any sisters.
She **has** a brother.	She **doesn't have** any sisters.
We _____ two sisters.	We _____ any brothers.
They _____ two sisters.	They _____ any brothers.

Questions	Short answers
Do you **have** a sister?	Yes, I **do**. No, I _____.
Does he/she **have** a sister?	Yes, he/she **does**. No, he/she **doesn't**.
_____ they **have** sisters?	Yes, they _____. No, they _____.
How many brothers **do** they _____?	Three.

- The present singular form of *have* is _____.
- Use _____ with singular subjects.
- Use _____ with plural subjects.
- Use *do + have* in questions with _____ subjects.
- Use _____ + _____ in questions with singular subjects.
- You can also use *has* or *have* for physical descriptions, for example, to describe eyes, hair, feet, hands, etc.

*I **have** brown eyes.*   *She **has** long, curly hair.*
*You **have** big feet!*   *We **have** small hands.*

Lesson 4C, page 35

Prepositions of time: *in*, *on*

in July
in (the) summer
in 2011
in the morning
in the afternoon
in the evening
on July 17
on Monday

Questions about time	Answers
When's your birthday?	It's **in** July. It's **on** Friday.
What day is your birthday?	It's **on** Friday.
What time is the party?	It's at 10.

- Use the preposition _____ with months, seasons, or years.
- Use _____ with time of the day (for example, morning, afternoon, evening).
- Use _____ with specific dates.
- Use _____ with specific days of the week.

5 Occupations

Complete the examples and the grammar rules that follow.

Lesson 5A, page 41 and Lesson 5B, page 43

Simple present

Affirmative	Negative
I **work** there.	I **don't work** here.
He **works** there.	He **doesn't work** here.
She **works** there.	She **doesn't work** here.
It **works** well.	It **doesn't work** well.
You **work** there.	You _____ _____ here.
We _____ there.	We _____ _____ here.
They _____ there.	They _____ _____ here.

- Use the simple present to tell facts.
  *My teacher **works** hard.*
- In affirmative statements, use the base form of a verb with *I*, _____, *we*, and _____.
- In simple present statements with singular subjects (except *I* and *You*), add *-s* or *-es* to the verb.
  *She **speaks** four languages.*
  *Mario usually **goes** to school early.*
- The long form of *doesn't* is _____.
- The short form, or contraction, of *do not* is _____.

Lesson 5A, page 41 and Lesson 5B, page 43

Questions	Short answers
_____ you **work** there?	Yes, I _____.
	No, I _____.
Does he **work** there?	Yes, he/she _____.
Does she **work** there?	No, he/she _____.
_____ we/they _____ there?	Yes, we/they **do**.
	No, we/they **don't**.
What do you **do**?	I'm a student.
What does she **do**?	She's a teacher.
Where do they **study**?	At Colegio Sta. Maria.
What languages **does** he **speak**?	Spanish and English.

- For *yes/no* questions with plural subjects (including *I* and *You*), use _____ + subject + the base form of a verb.
- In information questions, use a question word + *do* or *does* + the _____ form of a verb.

Lesson 5C, page 45

Subject pronouns	Object pronouns
I	He likes **me**.
you	He likes **you**.
he	She likes **him**.
she	He likes **her**.
it	We like **it**.
we	They like **us**.
they	We like **them**.

- Subject and object pronouns replace _____.
- _____ pronouns usually come after the verb in a sentence.
- The pronoun _____ is both singular and plural.

6 Daily Life

Complete the examples and the grammar rules that follow.

Lesson 6A, page 49

Simple present with fixed times
Preposition of time: *at*

Questions	Answers
What time **does** it **start**?	It **starts at** 11:30 A.M.
What time _____ the games **end**?	They _____ at 10 P.M.

Verbs usually followed by fixed times
start   end   open   close   arrive   leave

- In itineraries and schedules, use the _____ tense to refer to actions that are planned and are not likely to change.

*The concert **starts at** 8 P.M.*
*The first express train **leaves at** 8:05 every morning.*

Lesson 6B, page 51

Adverbs of frequency

I **always** get up early.
I **usually** get up early.
I **often** get up early.
She **sometimes** gets up late.
She **hardly ever** gets up late.
She **never** gets up late.

Positions of frequency adverbs

After the verb *be*	Before other verbs
I**'m sometimes** late for school.	I **sometimes** <u>get up</u> late.

- Use adverbs of frequency with the _____ tense.
- Adverbs of frequency come _____ the verb *be*.
- They come _____ other verbs.

Lesson 6C, page 53

How often/Adverbial expressions of frequency

How often do you get up early?
I get up early **every day**.

Common expressions of frequency

every (day/week/month)
once (a day/week/month/year)
twice (a day/week/month/year)
three times (a day/week/month/year)
several times (a day/week/month/year)
once in a while

Positions of the adverbial phrase

- **Every weekend**, I go to the gym.
  (before a sentence)
- I go to the gym **every weekend**.
  (after a sentence)

- Use the question words _____ to ask about the frequency of activities.
- Adverbial expressions of frequency can come at the beginning or _____ of a sentence.

Complete the examples and the grammar rules that follow.

Lesson 7A, page 59

Can (present ability)

Affirmative	Negative
I/You **can** dance.	I/You **can't** sing.
He/She **can** dance.	He/She **can't** sing.
We/They **can** dance.	We/They **can't** sing.

Questions	Short answers
Can you dance?	Yes, I **can**.
	No, I _____.

Contraction
cannot = **can't**

- *Can* + verb expresses present ability.
- The verb after *can* is always in the _____ form.
- For *yes/no* questions with *can*, the word order is *Can* + subject + _____.

Lesson 7B, page 61

Count nouns	Noncount nouns
bananas	bread
cookies	rice
potatoes	water

Some in affirmative statements

There are **some** eggs in the bowl.
There's **some** milk in the refrigerator.

Any in questions and negative statements

There aren't **any** eggs in the refrigerator.
There isn't **any** milk in the refrigerator.
Are there **any** eggs?

- Count nouns are nouns that we can easily count. They have singular and plural forms. *Singular* means _____; _____ means "more than one."
- _____ nouns cannot be counted. For example, we can't count *water*, so *water* is noncount.

- Use _____ before plural nouns and noncount nouns in affirmative statements.
  *There are **some** cookies in the fridge.*
- Use _____ before plural nouns and noncount nouns in *yes/no* questions and negative statements.
  *Are there **any** cookies left?*
  *There aren't **any** left.*

Lesson 7C, page 62

Imperatives

Affirmative	Negative
Say cheese.	**Don't** move!

- Use the imperative for instructions, directions, or requests.
  ***Go** to page 12.*
  ***Turn** left.*
  *Please, **close** the window.*
- Use the _____ form of a verb for the imperative.
- Use _____, or ***do not***, for the negative imperative.

Lesson 7C, page 63

Prepositions of place

My house is **near** my school.
Her house is **across from** the park.
Their house is **between** the park **and** the bank.
His house is **on the corner of** Diego and Luna Streets.

Using prepositions with addresses

in + name of country or city
in + room number
on + name of street or road
at + building number
on the + floor (in a building)
on the corner of + name of street

- *Across from* means "on the opposite side."
- Use a _____ + noun to say where something is.

8 Free time

Complete the examples and the grammar rules that follow.

Lesson 8A, page 67

Present continuous

Affirmative	Negative
I'm texting my friend.	I'm not e-mailing him.
He's texting his friends.	He isn't/He's not e-mailing his friends.
She___ _____ her friends.	She isn't/She___ _____ _____ her friends.
You're texting your friend.	You aren't/You___ _____ _____ your friend.
We___ _____ our friends.	We aren't/We're not e-mailing our friends.
They___ _____ their friends.	They aren't/They___ _____ _____ their friends.

Questions	Short answers
Are you texting him?	Yes, I am./No, I'm not.
_____ he _____ her?	Yes, he _____. No, he___ _____.
What are you doing?	I'm texting.

- Use the present continuous to talk about an activity that is happening or not happening right now.
  We're studying English this year.
  We're not studying French.
- The present continuous form is *is/am/are* + verb ending in _____.
- Follow these spelling rules to change the base form into *-ing* form:

  Group 1 Consonant + *-e*: Drop the *-e* and add *-ing*.
  write → writing

  Group 2 One vowel + one consonant: double the consonant and add *-ing*.
  sit → sitting

  Group 3 Two vowels + one consonant: Add *-ing*; do not double the consonant.
  read → reading

Lesson 8B, page 69

Simple present	Present continuous
I **play** basketball twice a week.	I'm **playing** basketball right now.
He/She **plays** basketball twice a week	He's/She's **playing** basketball right now.
We/They **play** basketball twice a week.	We're/They're **playing** basketball right now.

- Use the _____ to talk about habits or routines, regular occurrences, or facts.
- Use the _____ to talk about an action that is happening now or these days.

Lesson 8C, page 71

Like, love, hate, prefer + -ing

Other verbs used with gerunds (verb + *-ing*)

enjoy	finish
start	keep

I **enjoy reading**.
I **started** _____ (read) it yesterday.
I **finished** _____ (read) it yesterday.
I **keep thinking** about you.

- A _____ is a verbal that ends in *-ing* and functions as a noun (that is, as subject and object) in a sentence.
  Listening to music relaxes me. (subject)
  I love listening to music. (object)

9 Past events

Complete the examples and the grammar rules that follow.

Lesson 9A, page 77

Simple past of *be*

Affirmative	Negative
I **was** at the concert last night.	I **wasn't** at the movies.
You **were** at the concert, too.	You **weren't** at the movies.
He/She _____ at the concert.	He/She _____ at the movies.
We **were** at the concert.	We **weren't** at the movies.
They _____ at the concert.	They _____ at the movies.

Questions	Short answers
Was he there, too?	Yes, he **was**. No, he **wasn't**.
Were they there, too?	Yes, they **were**. No, they **weren't**.
Where **were** you?	At the concert.
When **was** the concert?	Last night.

- The simple past forms of *be* are _____ and _____.
- Use _____ with singular subjects; use _____ with *you* and with plural subjects.
- Use past-time expressions with the simple past.

Lesson 9B, page 79

Simple past of regular verbs

Affirmative

I, He/She, You, We/They

walked out of the house last night.

Negative

I, He/She, You, We/They

didn't walk out of the house last night.

Simple past of regular verbs

Simple past verb endings of regular verbs

notice = noticed; walk = walked; carry = carried

Contraction

did not = **didn't**

- Use the _____ to talk about activities that are finished at a specific time in the past.
- The simple past form of regular verbs end in _____, *-ed*, or *-ied*.
- For negative statements in the simple past, use *did + not +* the _____ form of a verb.

Lesson 9B, page 79

Prepositions of motion: *across, along, down, up, into, out of, past*

To get to the restaurant, walk **along** the river until you get to the bridge. Then go **across** the bridge and make a left on State Street.
The bride-to-be practiced walking **down** the aisle.
Walk **up** those stairs, and you'll see a red door.
We walked **into** the scary house and ran **out of** it immediately.
I walk **past** his house every morning on my way to school.

- Prepositions of motion express movement toward or away from something.

Lesson 9C, page 80

Simple past of regular verbs

Questions	Short answers
Did you **practice** yesterday?	Yes, I **did**./No, I **didn't**.
When did you **practice**?	Yesterday.
Where _____ you practice?	At the school playground.

- For *yes/no* questions, use: _____ + subject + the base form of a verb.
- For information questions, use: a question word + _____ subject + the base form of a verb.

10 Travel

Complete the examples and the grammar rules that follow.

Lesson 10A, page 85

Simple past of irregular verbs

Affirmative	Negative
I **went** on vacation last summer.	I **didn't go** on vacation. last summer.
You **went** on vacation. last summer.	You **didn't go** on vacation last summer.
He _____ on vacation last summer.	He _____ _____ on vacation last summer.
She _____ on vacation last summer.	She _____ _____ on vacation last. summer
We _____ on vacation last summer.	We _____ _____ on vacation last summer.
They _____ on vacation last summer.	They _____ _____ on vacation last summer.

Partial list of irregular verbs

Base form	Simple past
be	**was, were**
buy	**bought**
get up	**got up**
go	**went**
find	**found**
have	**had**
make	**made**
run	**ran**
see	**saw**
sit	**sat**

- Irregular past verbs do not end in *-d* or *-ed*. Their past form varies.
- Use the _____ form of a verb with *did* and *didn't*.
  She **didn't** sleep well last night.
  We **didn't** sleep well last night.

Simple past of irregular verbs: Questions

Questions	Answers
Did you **have** a good time?	Yes, I **did**. No, I **didn't**.
_____ he _____ a good time?	Yes, he _____. No, he _____.
_____ they _____ a good time?	Yes, they _____. No, they _____.
What **did** you **do**? What _____ he _____?	I went hiking. He went hiking.

Lesson 10C, page 89

Simple past with *ago*

We went to Teotihuacan a year **ago**.

Some past-time expressions

(several/a few) minutes/hours ago
(several/a few) days/weeks/months/years ago
an hour ago
a or one minute/day/week/month/year ago

- Past-time expressions can come at the end or at the beginning of statements.
  *We were at a concert **a week ago**.*
  ***A week ago** we were at a concert.*
- They are usually at the end of questions.
  *Where were you **a week ago**?*

11 Choices

Complete the examples and the grammar rules that follow.

Lesson 11A, page 95

Comparative and superlative of short adjectives
Comparative
My cell phone is **smaller than** yours.
Superlative
Polly's cell phone is **the smallest** of all three.

- Use the comparative form to compare two people, two places, or two things.
- The comparative form of most short adjectives ends in -er + _____.
- Use the superlative form to compare three or more people, places, or things.
- To form the superlative of short adjectives, use *the* before the adjective and add _____.

Lesson 11B, page 97

Comparative and superlative of long adjectives	
Comparative	**Superlative**
more famous than	the most famous
_____ beautiful	_____
_____	_____ beautiful

- To form the superlative of long adjectives, use *the* + _____ before the adjective.
- After the superlative, use a prepositional phrase such as *in the world (on earth), of all,* or *of all the . . .* *The hottest* place on earth is El Azizia in Libya.

Lesson 11C, page 98

Which + indefinite pronoun: *one/ones*
A: I like that belt.
B: Which **one**?
A: This **one**. OR That **one**.
A: I like those jeans.
B: Which **ones**?
A: Those. OR The dark-blue **ones**.
NOTE: Do not say "these ones" or "those ones."

- Use *one* in place of a _____ count noun.
- Use *ones* in place of _____ count nouns.
- Use *one* after *this* and _____.
- Do not use *ones* after *these* and *those*.

12 Big events

Complete the examples and the grammar rules that follow.

Lesson 12A, page 103

Be going to + verb for future plans and intentions

Affirmative	Negative
I'm going to celebrate tonight.	I'm not going to study tonight.
He's/She's going to celebrate tonight.	He's/She's not going to study.
We're/They're going to celebrate tonight.	We're/They're not going to study.

Questions	Short answers
_____ you _____ to celebrate tonight?	Yes, I _____./ No, I'm _____.
What ____ you _____ do tonight?	I'___ _____ to celebrate.

- *Be going to* + verb expresses future activities.
- Use _____ + base form to talk about plans and intentions.

Lesson 12B, page 105

Possessive pronouns

Possessive adjectives	Possessive pronouns
My idea was good.	Mine was good.
Her idea was good.	_____ was good.
His idea was good.	His was good.
Your idea was good.	_____ was good.
Their idea was good.	_____ was good.

Whose . . . ?

A: **Whose** coat is this?
B: It's Jenny's. OR It's **hers**.

- Possessive _____ replace a possessive adjective and a noun.
- Use the question word _____ to ask about possessions.
Whose book is this?

Lesson 12C, page 106

Want + infinitive

Some verbs followed by infinitive		
agree	hope	prefer
decide	need	try
expect	plan	

- An infinitive consists of *to* + the base form of a verb.
I agreed **to help** *her.*
- The verbs *like*, *love*, and *hate* can be followed by a gerund or an infinitive.
She likes **cooking**. (gerund)
She likes **to cook**. (infinitive)

CLIL PROJECTS

CLIL Project 1D, page 11
Social studies

Make a list of friends and relatives from different countries who are studying or have studied English. List their names, ages, grade levels, and nationalities. Go to the above website, look for CLIL Project 1D, and print out the instructions.

CLIL Project 2D, page 19
Ethics

PAIRS/GROUPS Talk about the different things you and your classmates do to remember and honor your mother on Mother's Day or your father on Father's Day. Make notes. Go to the above website, look for CLIL Project 2D, and print out the instructions.

CLIL Project 3D, page 29
Social studies

PAIRS/GROUPS Brainstorm the types of houses found in different parts of the world. List them. Go to the above website, look for CLIL Project 3D, and print out the instructions.

CLIL Project 4D, page 37
Biology

PAIRS/GROUPS Discuss: What are multiple births? What types of multiple births do you know? List them. Go to the above website, look for CLIL Project 4D, and print out the instructions.

CLIL Project 5D, page 47
Ethics

GROUPS List five places in your town that you and your friends go to. Talk about some of the things you do in each of these places. Include both right and wrong things. Then go to the above website, look for CLIL Project 5D, and print out the instructions.

CLIL Project 6D, page 55
Social studies

PAIRS Talk about your weekend routines. What time do you get up? List all the activities you do throughout the day. Then go to the above website, look for CLIL Project 6D, and print out the instructions.

CLIL Project 7D, page 65
Science; Health and physical education

GROUPS List the food items available in your school cafeteria. Discuss: Does your school cafeteria offer healthful food? Which foods are healthful? Which foods are junk food? Go to the above website, look for CLIL Project 7D, and print out the instructions.

CLIL Project 8D, page 73
Art; English

GROUPS Plan the design of a website for teenagers. What elements will it have? What topics will you include? Go to the above website, look for CLIL Project 8D, and print out the instructions.

CLIL Project 9D, page 83
Science; Technology

GROUPS Examine a new cell phone. What are its features? What applications and functionalities does it have? Design a cell phone for the future. Go to the above website, look for CLIL Project 9D, and print out the instructions.

CLIL Project 10D, page 91
Geography; Social studies

PAIRS Plan an imaginary trip to several countries for your class. Which countries will you travel to? Go to the above website, look for CLIL Project 10D, and print out the instructions.

CLIL Project 11D, page 101
Ethics

GROUPS Brainstorm common problems students have at school. List them. Rank them, with number 1 being the most serious. Then go to the above website, look for CLIL Project 11D, and print out the instructions.

CLIL Project 12D, page 109
Art; English

GROUPS Brainstorm fun events for your school or town. What does each event celebrate? Choose one and create a poster for the event. Go to the above website, look for CLIL Project 12D, and print out the instructions.